Rosalie E Youngdahl

Chief Justice Marshall

THE SHORT CONSTITUTION

ELEMENTARY AMERICANISM SERIES

BEING A CONSIDERATION OF THE CONSTITUTION
OF THE UNITED STATES, WITH PARTICULAR
REFERENCE TO THE GUARANTIES OF LIFE,
LIBERTY, AND PROPERTY CONTAINED THEREIN,
SOMETIMES DESIGNATED THE BILL OF RIGHTS

BY

MARTIN J. WADE

Judge of the United States District Court

AND

WILLIAM F. RUSSELL

Dean of the College of Education, State University of Iowa

ANNOTATIONS BY

CHARLES H. MEYERHOLZ

Professor of Social Science, Iowa State Teachers College

Third and Revised Edition

———

AMERICAN CITIZEN PUBLISHING CO.
IOWA CITY

ELEMENTARY AMERICANISM SERIES

By Martin J. Wade and William F. Russell
Annotations by Charles H. Meyerholz

THE SHORT CONSTITUTION
Third and Revised Edition. Price, $1.50
(Ready)

AUTHORITY AND OBEDIENCE
THE MAKING OF A LAW
THE SERVANTS OF THE PEOPLE
(In Preparation)

LESSONS IN AMERICANISM
By Martin J. Wade
(In Preparation)

AMERICAN CITIZEN PUBLISHING CO.
IOWA CITY

What Has America Done For Me And For My Children **?**

THIS question may not be spoken, but it is in the hearts of millions of Americans to-day.

All those who attempt to teach Americanism to foreigners, *and to Americans,* must be prepared *to answer this question. It can only be answered* by teaching the individual guaranties of the Constitution of the United States, and of the States, which protect life and liberty and property.

It can only be answered by convincing the people that this is a land of justice and of opportunity for all; that if there be abuses, they are due not to our form of government, but that the people are themselves to blame, because of their ignorance of their rights, their failure to realize their power, and their neglect of those duties which citizenship imposes.

All over the land earnest men and women are endeavoring to teach the great truths of Americanism, and with substantial success; but those who understand human nature realize that the faith of our fathers can only be firmly established by lighting the fires of patriotism and loyalty in the hearts of our children. Through them the great truths of our National life can be brought into the homes of the land.

And the Nation will never be safe until the Constitution is carried into the homes, until at every fireside young and old shall feel a new sense of security in the guaranties which are found in this great charter of human liberty, and a new feeling of gratitude for the blessings which it assures to this, and to all future generations.

TABLE OF CONTENTS

ABOUT THE AUTHORS

FOR a work designed to promote education in the spirit of American citizenship it would be difficult to imagine a more competent authorship than that which has been provided for "The Short Constitution". Either of the writers alone would have produced a book of high standing in this field; the collaboration of the two makes it a remarkable production in its adaptation to the subject for home reading, the study club, and the school curriculum. It is unique, and has justly been termed "the first real attempt to popularize Constitutional law".

Federal Judge Martin J. Wade has had a varied contact with people in his long experience as practicing attorney, district judge, member of Congress, and Judge of the United States Court. A well known Iowa publicist, he has gained nation wide fame as a public speaker and writer on Americanization and citizenship topics, basing his themes on first-hand experiences with conditions which have produced much unrest throughout the Nation. As a member of the State Council of National Defense during the World War, and as presiding judge at the trial of many obstructionists in that period, he conceived the idea of the need for a school of Americanism, to teach what our country has done for its citizens. Clearness and eloquence mark his public addresses, and have enriched the arguments and illustrations of this first book of the "Elementary Americanism Series".

Dean William F. Russell was the educational adviser sent with a group of experts by appointment of the President of the United States to advise disorganized Russia during the latter part of the World War; and also one of the five members of the China Educational Commission of North America, sent to China in 1921. His course of study in American citizenship, written at the request of the National Masonic Research Society for use throughout the United States, was inspired by the observation that the government in Russia, in contrast with our own, was an agency that took money for its coffers and boys for its armies and gave nothing in return. In addition to his work as Dean of the College of Education of the State University of Iowa, and his record as a widely-known lecturer on educational topics, he has found time to write school texts notable for accurate and concise statement, adapted to arousing and sustaining interest in the student mind.

The authors have done more than present the facts about the Constitution of the United States, with particular emphasis on its personal guaranties. They have vitalized a topic generally thought to be dry and technical. They have succeeded in making the Constitution seem to be what it is, a factor of first importance in the daily life of the average citizen. It is not too much to say that the seed of this book should be planted in every home in America.

The admirable work of annotation by Professor Chas. H. Meyerholz, Professor of Social Science in the Iowa State Teachers College, gives much additional material for elementary and advanced study. Professor Meyerholz is well known as an authoritative teacher, writer, and lecturer on subjects pertaining to government, and has done much valuable Americanization work.

The elementary and advanced questions at the end of each chapter will serve as a guide to all teachers and leaders of study classes. The text of the Declaration of Independence and the Constitution of the United States, with the original capitalization and punctuation preserved, and an abridgement of a State Constitution, printed at the end of the book, are valuable for reference.

THE PUBLISHER

PREFACE

"THE SHORT CONSTITUTION" is one of a series of volumes entitled "Elementary Americanism", intended for use in the home, the club, the school, and in general Americanization work.

It is our hope that regular courses in "Americanism" will soon be established in all schools, colleges, and universities.

We use the term "Americanism" because we feel that it signifies something broader, deeper, and more appealing than any title now used in the schools in the teaching of American government, or citizenship, or the rights and duties of the citizens of the United States.

We like the term "America" better than "the United States". "The United States" suggests boundaries, codes, and constitutions. "America" suggests all these and then it suggests *spirit*. There *is* such a thing as "Americanism". It includes all there is of information relating to our country; but it also has a soul. "Americanism" relates to democracy, into which enter all the ideals, all the impulses and emotions of men, women, and children. "Americanism" teaches not only the relation of the States to the National government, and the relation of citizens to both the State and the National government, but it also teaches the relation of men, women, and children to each other.

This is a government by the people, and therefore we must understand the people in order that we, the people, may govern.

To arouse patriotism and loyalty we must do more than develop the powers of the mind, do more than expand the field of knowledge. We must inspire in the heart faith, confidence, and love. Men must not only learn how to govern, but they must learn how to be governed. We must not only learn to command, but also to obey. Our spirits must be so

9

molded that we can submit to duly constituted authority, submission to which is the most lofty expression of American patriotism.

Submission to authority in America is submission to law, for no man in this country has any authority to command or direct a fellowman, except as the law made by the people vests him with such authority.

To inspire devotion to our country we must arouse in the hearts of our people a sense of gratitude for the blessings which come to us because we live in free America, gratitude for the rights and liberties which we possess, which are protected by the guaranties of a written Constitution adopted by the people themselves.

There is only one way in which the average person may be brought to see what America has done for him, and that is by contrasting the rights, privileges, and opportunities which he has with those possessed by others in the same walk of life before the Constitution became the bulwark of the people against injustice and wrong.

The aim of "The Short Constitution" is to present, in a form as simple as possible, a definite knowledge of all the personal guaranties of the Constitution, with an explanation of what they mean, and what they have done in the advancement of human happiness; and a brief explanation of the machinery of government provided by the Constitution.

Everyone who understands human nature will admit that to mold the spirit, to inspire faith, and to excite gratitude training must begin in childhood. The child must learn:

(a) What authority means.

(b) The source of authority.

(c) In whom authority rests: in the parent, in the teacher, and in public officers selected by the people to enforce the authority of the community, the State, and of the Nation.

(d) How the authority of the people, the community, the State, and the Nation is expressed through laws which are nothing but rules of human conduct.

(e) How we should respect authority and submit to authority.

(f) How and by whom those who will not yield obedience to authority out of respect will be compelled to obey by punishment.

We have adopted a new method of presenting this subject. In this country authority is largely administered through the courts. Judges of the courts construe the Constitution and the laws; and, generally with the aid of a jury, determine rights and wrongs, and enforce justice through their judgments and decrees.

We therefore feel that the subject "Americanism", presented through the spoken word of a judge, will better gain and hold the attention of the pupil than in any other way. We have the teacher invite Judge Garland to deliver a series of "Talks" to the pupils, which are herein presented. By this direct method greater freedom of expression is permitted and with the aid of notes greater brevity is possible. In these "Talks" considerable apparent repetition will appear. This is essential to thorough understanding. Without reiteration it is impossible to accomplish our purpose which is not only to enlighten, but to inspire.

Our endeavor is to present the subject not from the standpoint of the government, but from the standpoint of the people. The *rights of the people* are of first importance in a Nation where men, women, and children are free. The State and the Nation have no rights except those given them by the people. Strictly speaking the Nation and the States have no "rights" but only the duty to exercise certain powers in the protection of the liberties of the people.

In America the rights of the people are supreme. The state exists for man, not man for the state.

To gain substantial results we must rely largely upon the industry and enthusiasm of the instructors. We are sure they will realize that in the "upbuilding of the spirit" a proper atmosphere must be created and maintained. Doctor Steiner wisely said, "Religion cannot be taught, it must be caught." In other words religion is of the spirit; so is patriotism. *Always bear in mind that in presenting the Constitution we are teaching human rights under the Constitution.*

It is more than a century since the Constitution was ratified, and, so far as we have knowledge, this is the first direct attempt to translate its guaranties into the language of the ordinary man, woman, and child. We demand respect for, and loyalty to the Constitution, but the truth is that the ordinary citizen has no knowledge of the relation of the Constitution to his life or to the life of his children.

THE AUTHORS

I

THE JUDGE'S FIRST TALK

REASONS FOR THE STUDY OF THE CONSTITUTION OF THE UNITED STATES

For several days there had been an air of expectancy about the school. At Monday's assembly the teacher had announced that she had persuaded Judge Garland to come to talk to the teachers and pupils about the Constitution of their country and about the law, the rights, the powers, and the duties of the people. A real live judge was coming! Most of the children had never seen a judge. The word inspired a sort of dread. They had read of men being sentenced to prison. They expected to see a fierce, hard-hearted man. Some of the younger children had wondered if it would be possible to stay away from the assembly room when the judge was there, but the teacher said that everyone should be present. So important was the subject that the teachers were to be there, too; and many fathers and mothers that could spare the time were also invited. The principal had said that he would not miss a meeting.

So when Friday came the assembly room was crowded. All the pupils and teachers were there, and in the rear of the room were a few of the parents. The door opened and the principal of the school entered. By his side was a man whose gray hair and serious countenance told of years of responsibility. He did not appear "fierce". Rather his face was kind and his eyes twinkled as he ascended the platform and stood looking out over the faces before him.

The principal introduced Judge Garland who bowed and began his series of talks to the children.

Well my friends, I am glad to see you. I am delighted to be

back in a school room again. It is many years ago, though it seems but a short time, since as a schoolboy I sat in a school room like this, among boys and girls like you. I suppose that I studied about as you study, and did not recite any better than you recite. I thought I had to work very hard, and I remember that I often looked out of the open window of the school room when the summer sun was warm, and I thought I could hear the trees, the grass, the stream, and even the fish calling me to quit study and come out to joy and freedom. I know it was a real temptation. I could have had a good time, but I have often been glad since that I obeyed my teacher, my parents, and the law, and continued my studies in school. I am glad, because I now realize how much easier, how much happier, and how much more useful my life has been because I did not listen to the voice of temptation which called me from work to play.[1]

Since those pleasant school days I have seen much of human life. On the bench now for over twenty-five years, I have been compelled to deal with all sorts of people, even the little children who early in life sometimes drift from the path of right to ways of wickedness. I have served as judge of the Juvenile Court, and judge of the court in which the worst criminals are tried. I have heard the cases of thousands of persons on trial for crimes, men and women, young and old. I have sent hundreds to prison, and I have been compelled to sentence some to death.

In this experience, I have learned something of how easy it is, unless we are on our guard, to sin against the laws of our country, and against the laws of God. I have observed that the average person does not fully appreciate the value of liberty until he is about to lose it.[2]

I also know that most people do not know the worth of the protection which our Constitution gives to each one of us, until someone is about to take away their right to life, or to liberty, or to property; and then they cry out for help. If they are right in their appeal, they always find help in the Constitution and in the law of the land. Yet it is true that there is much real ignorance about our country, our Constitution, and our laws. There is even much ignorance of these things among people who are supposed to be well educated.

So I was pleased when your teacher came to me the other day asking me to come to your school a couple of times a week, to talk to you about our country, our Constitution, and our laws. I am happy to be able to comply with her request. It is a difficult subject for children, yet children must study these things, and learn them. There is no more important subject.[3]

One of the chief objects of furnishing free education to children, rich and poor, is to make of them good law-abiding citizens; citizens who know what authority is; citizens who will obey the voice of authority; citizens who realize that authority in this country rests in the people themselves; citizens, men and women, who realize that they owe a duty to their country and their fellowmen to do all they can to keep America the most free and the most just country in the world.[4]

No American child should leave school without a full knowledge of the government of our country; nor until he has in his heart loyal devotion to America, and to the Stars and Stripes, the emblem of the free.

Of course I do not expect you to learn all there is to be known about your government. However I do expect you to know the great fundamental truths which after all are very simple and easily understood.

I am not endeavoring to make lawyers. I am not trying to train you to become lawyers. You know nearly all the children in the American schools have to learn something about physiology and hygiene, but not in order to become doctors. They study physiology and hygiene in order to

understand the ordinary rules of health, so that they may
protect themselves as far as possible against disease and take
care of their bodies intelligently. Of course sickness will
come. Then you must call the doctor.

Well, so it is in this course. I want you to know enough
about your government, your Constitution, and your laws—
because these things are yours—so that you, as members of
this great society called America, will be able to understand
your rights and duties, your privileges, your opportunities,
and your obligations. Sometime in your life your problem
may become so difficult, or your rights may become so en-
dangered, that you will have to call upon a lawyer, just as
when illness comes you call upon your physician.[5]

No one knows anything of real worth about his country
until he knows its Constitution. No one can have in his heart
a full measure of gratitude for the blessings of living in a free
country, until he knows of how fully the Constitution guards
every right and privilege which we hold dear. So we shall
enter upon the study of the Constitution of our country.

But in order that you may better understand the Constitution of your country, in order that you may better study
the problems which will be presented to you in this course,
it is necessary for you to understand something, in a general
way at least, of four separate things—*Government, Liberty,
Authority,* and *Law.* So before talking to you of the Constitution, I shall talk to you on these subjects.[6]

I know it will not be easy for you at first to understand
some of the words and expressions which it is necessary for
me to use. It will be necessary for me to repeat to some extent, from time to time, but I feel satisfied that if we will
work together in the right spirit, you will find the matter interesting; and I am sure that the great truths, the great principles of life, conduct, and action will soon become clear to
your minds.

The important thing to realize at all times is that we are not talking about something away off in which we have slight interest, but that we are talking of things which are ours, which affect every one of us, not in the future, but now.

I can recall a number of faces of men who have been before my court charged with crimes, who in childhood were sitting where you are sitting to-day. I have sentenced some of them to long terms of years in the penitentiary. I was compelled to take away from them their liberty, because they had shown themselves unworthy, and had shown themselves rebels against the authority of their country.

On the other hand, I recall those who came into court seeking protection of their rights against wrongdoers—against those who would take away their property, the earnings perhaps of a lifetime; and in court they found protection, justice, and right. But in administering justice and right, the court was only applying the principles of the Constitution of our country which we are about to study.

So let us enter upon this work with a determination to succeed in our undertaking. You know that has a great deal to do with our success in life—a determination to succeed.

When you boys take your baseball team to play the team of some other school, you start for the baseball park determined to win the game; and, if you keep up this spirit, you probably will win the game. In any event, you play a real game of which your friends are proud. That is the way to meet all the problems of life, whether in the school room, or out in the world after you have entered upon the great battles of life.

NOTES AND COMMENTS

1. Boys and girls often do not realize the value of an education as a preparation for success in life. The following figures from an educational authority show what education does for a boy or a girl.

(a) Less than three per cent of the people of the United States have a college education, but this three per cent furnishes fifty-nine per cent of the men and women called successful. Fourteen per cent come from those having had some college training. This shows that nearly three-fourths of all men and women in the United States called successful have had some college training.

(b) During the past ten years Massachusetts has given all her children a minimum of seven years of schooling, while Tennessee has given her children but three years. The Massachusetts citizens produce per capita $260 per year, while the Tennessee citizens produce per capita $116 per year.

(c) Of the fifty-five members attending the Federal convention that made the Constitution of the United States in 1787, thirty had attended college, and twenty-six had college degrees. Of the forty State officers in Iowa in 1918, thirty were college graduates, seven were graduates of high schools, and only three had less than a high school education.

(d) The child with no schooling has one chance in 150,000 of performing distinguished services; with elementary education he has four times the chance; with high school education he has eighty-seven times the chance; with college education he has eight hundred times the chance.

(e) Every boy and every girl should stick to his school work until he at least graduates from a fully accredited high school.

2. "Law can do nothing without morals."—Benjamin Franklin.

"Through the whole of life and the whole system of duties, much the strongest moral obligations are such as were never the results of our option."—Edmund Burke.

"To do evil that good may come of it, is for the bungler in politics as well as in morals."—Benjamin Franklin.

"Duty is not collective; it is personal."—Calvin Coolidge.

3. "Ignorance of the law excuses no man."—Selected.

"Knowledge is in every country the surest basis of public happiness." —George Washington.

4. "The thorough education of all classes of people is the most efficacious means of promoting the prosperity of the Nation. The material interests of its citizens, as well as their moral and intellectual culture, depend upon its accomplishment."—Robert E. Lee.

"In a Republic education is indispensable. A Republic without education is like the creature of imagination, a human being without a soul, living and moving blindly, with no just sense of the present or the future."—Charles Sumner.

"Without popular education, no government which rests upon popular action can long endure. The people must be schooled in the knowledge, and if possible in the virtues, upon which the maintenance and success of free institutions depend."—Woodrow Wilson.

5. "Where the State has bestowed education, the man who accepts it must be content to accept it merely as charity, unless he returns it to the State in full in the shape of good citizenship."—Theodore Roosevelt.

6. "*Government—Liberty—Authority—Law*—the man or the woman who fails to appreciate the true meaning of these terms, lacks the training necessary to be a good citizen in a Republic."—Abraham Lincoln.

"We need more of the office desk and less of the show-window in politics. Let men in office substitute the midnight oil for the lime-light." —Calvin Coolidge.

ELEMENTARY QUESTIONS

1. Did you ever see a judge? Would you be afraid of a judge? Why?
2. What are the duties of a judge?

3. Why did the judge say, "But I have often been glad since, that I obeyed my teacher, my parents, and the law, and continued my studies in school"? Why do boys and girls go to school? Why is the public willing to pay large sums of money to pay teachers, buy books, build school buildings, and keep them open?

4. What law was it that the judge said he was glad that he had obeyed?

5. Why did the judge send hundreds to prison? Why was he compelled to sentence some to death?

6. What are the advantages of staying in school? What more do you know when you graduate from elementary school than those who quit earlier? Should one try to graduate from high school? Why?

7. The judge says that one of the chief purposes of school is to make good, law-abiding citizens. Think of some person you know who is a "good, law-abiding citizen"; think of some one who is not; name five ways in which they are different.

8. Have you read the Constitution of the United States? Should a good, law-abiding citizen know what is in the Constitution of the United States?

9. The judge says that we owe a duty to our country. List five duties that a school pupil owes to his father and mother, five that he owes to his teacher, and, if you can, list five duties that all of us owe to our country.

10. The judge says that the Constitution guards every right and privilege that we hold dear. Can you name any rights or privileges that you hold dear?

ADVANCED QUESTIONS

A. Why do we say that the United States is the "land of the free"? Why does the judge say that it is the most free and just country in the world?

B. How are judges selected? To whom are they responsible? What are their duties?

C. What are likely to be the results of poor schools?

D. Should a parent have a right to give a child as poor an education or as little schooling as he may desire?

E. Why do some States require children to study physiology and hygiene? Is there as good an argument for a study of the Constitution?

F. Why does the judge say, "No one knows anything of real worth about his country until he knows its Constitution"?

G. The judge says that good citizens know what authority is. Give an illustration of a child, a student, and a citizen who knows what authority is. Define authority. Give an illustration of a man who does not respect authority.

H. When is a country a "free country"? What is a "just country"? How can a judge justify himself in a free country when he sends some men to prison, thereby taking away their freedom?

I. How can an American protect his liberties? What steps must he take?

J. Prepare a paper on one of the following subjects:
    The Advantages of Staying in School
    One Law-abiding Citizen That I Know
    What One Man I Know Knows About the Rights and Privileges of the American Citizen Under the Constitution.
    Why Everyone Should Study the Constitution
    What a Law Is, Where It Comes From and Its Value

II

GOVERNMENT

THE PURPOSE AND ORIGIN OF GOVERNMENT AMONG MEN —IN THE UNITED STATES

It is a little difficult even for grown people to understand clearly what is meant by "the government". They have so many absurd notions about what the government is, and where it is, that I do not wonder that children do not understand. If I could look into the mind of each child here this morning, I am sure I would find many that picture the capitol at Washington, the President, or some other officer as being the government. Now the capitol and the President and the Congress and the Supreme Court of the United States and all other National officers are part of the government, *but they are not the government.*[1]

The government of the United States is merely the agency by which and through which the people protect their own rights and liberties. Our government may be said to be the organized will of all the people. The people govern in this country, and the men and the means by which they govern all combined may be said to be the government. But do not ever forget this fact: the President is not a master, but a servant. The President, Senators, congressmen, and judges, in the Nation; the Governors, State Senators, and State Representatives in the States are only agents or servants of the people to carry out the people's will. Also do not forget that the power of government does not rest in Washington, the capital of the Nation, nor at the capitals of the different States. The power of government exists all over these United States. The power of government exists right in the homes and hearts of the people.[2]

The President has no power except that conferred upon him by the Constitution and the laws which the people have adopted. Neither have the Senators, the congressmen, nor the judges any power except that given by the people, and the people at any time can take away any part of the power given. When I say the people, I mean of course all the people. Not that all the people must agree to any law to have it enacted. The majority of the people make the laws as a rule. We shall take this up later and consider it fully. Government is power to exercise authority. Authority is in the people, and the authority of the people is expressed as they want it in laws which they make.

But what is government for? Why have any government? Government is organized to protect human rights.[3] Perhaps if you were a giant possessed of wonderful wisdom you would not need any law to protect your rights because you would be big enough, powerful enough, and wise enough to resist any person who might undertake to interfere with your rights; but we are not all giants and we are not all wise. In fact there are very few giants in the world. It is true, however, that some are bigger and stronger than others; and sometimes these big, strong people are selfish, wicked, or envious. They see that a weaker person has something which they want, and being big and strong, if there were no law to restrain them, they would take it.

Now if you have a bicycle and some full-grown, strong, brutal man were to come into your yard, take your bicycle, and start away with it, what would you do? You might protest. You might beg him not to take your property, but this would probably do no good. A thief does not stop when he is asked to by the owner of the property he is stealing, nor is a thief influenced by the fact that his act is wrong. In fact doing wrong is the business of a thief.

So there being many strong people in the world and many

weak people, many wise people, and many simple people, the full grown and the children, and many, many people who are not guided by rules of right or morality or justice, you can see how necessary it is that someone shall provide rules and regulations under which the weak, the simple, and the young may be protected from the strong, the brutal, and the wicked who would deprive their neighbors of their rights or their property, simply because they had the power to do it. This is what the government does.

There have been times in the world, hundreds and thousands of years, during which the strong governed the weak, made the weak their slaves, took from the weak the earnings of their toil; but our government exists for the very purpose of restraining the strong and protecting the weak, so that their rights are equal. Every man is free and no man is a slave.

Therefore always keep in mind that the purpose of government is to protect the people of all classes and ages so that, so far as possible, all may be equal in their right to do the things they want to do, own the things they want to own so far as they are able to produce or procure them, think the things they want to think, and speak the things they want to speak. In other words, *government is to protect our freedom against the wrongs of others.*

Now we must not have the notion in our mind that the government has anything to do with who shall work, or who shall play, or who shall idle. Occupations in life are not selected by the government. Each person determines this for himself. That is one of the privileges which we have in a free country, to select our own occupations; and as you go through life you will find that what appear to be the higher or better occupations are usually earned by industry, faithfulness, and honesty.[4]

I am going to talk to you some day about occupations in

life so that you will understand that our place in life is selected by ourselves, determined by our efforts and our conduct. I want you to start out in life with such a knowledge of these things that you will never blame your country if you do not like your job.

But how did our government come into existence? What was the beginning? Well, it is all very simple if we only get right down to elementary principles, if we only "begin at the beginning". Perhaps your father is a Woodman, or an Odd Fellow, or a Knight of Columbus. Perhaps he is a member of the American Federation of Labor. Perhaps your mother belongs to the Eastern Star, or the P. E. O. society. Perhaps you belong to some school fraternity, debating society, or neighborhood club, the Boy Scouts, or the Camp Fire Girls.

Now let us go back a few years. None of these societies were in existence. Where did they come from? One day, years ago, a few men and women, or boys and girls, met perhaps in some home, or the office, and talked over the plan which perhaps had been suggested by some one present at the meeting. After discussion, it was decided to form an organization. I have no doubt that most of you have had such an experience. The beginning of each society was merely an idea in the mind of some one. He or she talked of it to some one else, and the discussion extended until enough of interested persons came together to complete an organization and give it a name.

What was the first step in perfecting the society or organization? It was the preparation of a written statement of the purposes and principles of the organization, which is usually called a constitution. When the constitution was completed, usually by a committee, all those about to become members of the society met and talked it over. Changes probably were made and the constitution finally adopted. Probably some voted against it, but those who did vote against it recognized that they should be bound by the judgment and will of the majority.[5]

Laws, or by-laws, as they are generally called, were then adopted to govern the conduct of the members in their relation to each other and to the society. These by-laws have been amended from time to time ever since, and perhaps at all times some of the members have believed that the by-laws should be different, but they have submitted to the will of the majority.

So with the United States. There was a time less than one hundred and fifty years ago when there was no such thing on earth. A comparatively few men, representing the people of the former colonies, decided to form a Nation, and in the Constitutional Convention after months of discussion, the Constitution was adopted, and it was finally ratified by the people of the States. While many persons opposed some of the provisions of the Constitution, all submitted to the will of the majority.

Thereafter, rules of conduct called laws—in your society by-laws—were adopted, and from time to time changed and extended as circumstances seemed to demand. We are going to talk about these laws in a few days.

But *there is the whole story*. There is the simple beginning of this now great Nation, the most powerful on earth.

So you see there is nothing mysterious about the origin of our Constitution. There is nothing mysterious about the origin or the organization of this government. The important thing to bear in mind is that it was formed by the people for themselves. Humanity, after thousands of years, had reached a point where they refused longer to be governed by a king or similar ruler.

All this will become more clear to you as you understand something of the nature of liberty and of law.

NOTES AND COMMENTS

1.   "Government is the aggregate of authorities which rule a society."
"Government is that institution or aggregate of institutions by which society makes and carries out those rules of action which are necessary to enable men to live in a social state, or which are imposed upon the people forming that society by those who possess the power or authority of prescribing them."—Bouvier's *Law Dictionary*, Vol. I, p. 891.

2.   Government is the organized means and power that a State or Nation employs for the purpose of securing the rights of the people, and of perpetuating its own existence.

The real aim and purpose is well stated in the preamble to our Constitution when it says: "to form a more perfect Union, establish Justice, insure domestic Tranquility, provide for the common Defence, promote the general Welfare, and secure the blessings of Liberty to ourselves and our Posterity".

Government can never rise higher than the ideals of the people who compose the government. Good governments are the products of good people. Good governments can only exist where the people are intelligent and upright in character, and where each citizen is willing to guard the rights and privileges of others as well as those of himself.

"This government *of the people, by the people,* and *for the people,* shall not perish from the earth."—Abraham Lincoln.

3.   The object of government is to protect the citizens of a country and to promote their general welfare, and it is composed of the officials who care for the public interests of the citizens.

Under republican government, the weakest citizen enjoys the same rights and privileges as do the strongest citizens, the poorest have the same protection given to the richest, the most humble man or woman has a chance to become the head of his or her government and to lead the Nation among the most powerful Nations in the world.

"Brains and character rule the world. There were scores of men a hundred years ago who had more intellect than Washington. He outlives and overrides them all by the influence of his character."—Wendell Phillips.

"The true greatness of nations is in those qualities which constitute the greatness of the individual."—Charles Sumner.

4.   "There is always hope in a man that actually and honestly works. In idleness alone is there perpetual despair."—Thomas Carlyle.

"He that hath a trade hath an estate, and he that hath a calling hath an office of profit and honor."—Benjamin Franklin.

"If you have the great talents, industry will improve them; if moderate abilities, industry will supply their deficiencies."—Joshua Reynolds.

"Other nations have received their laws from conquerors; some are indebted for a constitution to the suffering of their ancestors through revolving centuries. The people of this country, alone, have formally and deliberately chosen a government for themselves, and with open and uninfluenced consent bound themselves into a social compact. Here no man proclaims his birth or wealth as a title to honorable distinction, or to sanctify ignorance and vice with the name of hereditary authority. He who has most zeal and ability to promote public felicity, let him be the servant of the public."—John Adams.

"The basis of our political system is the right of the people to make or alter their constitution of government."—George Washington.

"Let us then, fellow citizens, unite with one heart and one mind and labor for the welfare of the country."—Thomas Jefferson.

"The Declaration of Independence and the Constitution of the United States are parts of one consistent whole, founded upon one and the same theory of government,—that the people are the only legitimate source of power, and that all just powers of government are derived from the consent of the governed."—John Quincy Adams.

5. This description almost perfectly fits the making of the Mayflower Compact in the cabin of the ship Mayflower on November 11, 1620. Those Pilgrim Fathers drew up an agreement which was the first attempt at a written constitution in the New World. The Fundamental Orders of Connecticut, of 1638, are generally conceded to be the oldest real constitution in America.

ELEMENTARY QUESTIONS

1. What is the government of the United States? Why isn't the capitol at Washington the government? Why is it impossible to point out the government of the United States upon the map?
2. What is a servant? Describe a servant. Why does the judge say that the President of the United States is only a servant of the people?
3. Was the Kaiser a servant of the German people? Why not?
4. Where does the President get his power? Where do members of Congress get their power? Judges? The Sheriff? The Mayor?
5. If we do not like what our servants do, how can we control them?
6. What is government in a school? In a club? What would it be like if there were no government in either? Name five advantages of having a government.
7. Suppose that you were like Robinson Crusoe, except that five of you were shipwrecked. Would you form a government? Why?
8. If you were to write a constitution, what would you include?
9. Suppose that a man came into your yard and tried to steal your bicycle, what could you do to protect your rights?
10. Do all people do what they think is right? How can you tell what is right and wrong?

ADVANCED QUESTIONS

A. What is the purpose of government?
B. Why is it wrong for the great and powerful to govern the small and weak? Does might make right?
C. Which would be the better government, one based upon might makes right, or one based upon right makes might? Why?
D. How can right make might?
E. In a free country can the government prescribe what occupations in life the people must follow? How are the higher and better occupations acquired in America?
F. How did the American government come into being?
G. How would you organize a literary society? List the steps in detail. Would you have a constitution? What should be included in any constitution?
H. Discuss the effect of a sudden breakdown in government.
I. What were the first steps in the actual organization of the government of the United States?
J. Write a paper on:
   The Ways in Which the Postmaster, Superintendent of Schools, Sheriff, Coroner, or Judge Serves the People
   Why We Cannot Locate Our Government On the Map
   The Advantages of Having a Government
   What a Constitution Should Include

III

LIBERTY

DEFINITION OF LIBERTY AND THE HISTORICAL BACK-GROUND OF THE STRUGGLE FOR IT

I hope that we now all understand that the purpose of government is to maintain the liberty of the people. I wish that every child would learn from the Declaration of Independence the following:

"We hold these truths to be self-evident, that all men are created equal, that they are endowed by their Creator with certain unalienable Rights, that among these are Life, Liberty and the pursuit of Happiness. That to secure these rights, Governments are instituted among Men, deriving their just powers from the consent of the governed."[1]

This expresses the whole purpose of government—to secure the right to life, to liberty, and to happiness.

I suppose every child here would like to be rich some day. A great many people feel that riches bring happiness. The experience of men, however, is that riches more often bring disappointments, burdens, and grief.

What is the most valuable thing in the world? It is not money, lands, nor jewels. The most valuable thing in the world is human liberty. I do not believe that we, born here in America, realize the value of human liberty. It comes to us as a heritage. We accept it as we accept the sunlight, the springtime, the harvest. I am afraid that we seldom stop to recall the fact that the great blessing of human liberty, as we have it here in America, did not exist before our Nation was born. Always remember that there were thousands of years before our country came into being, when the people, men, women, and children living in many countries of the

world and under many forms of government dreamed,
hoped, and prayed for freedom. But it never came to them.
They lived, labored, and died under kings and emperors, or
other rulers, never having any power, or at most very limited
power, in making the laws under which they were compelled
to live.[2]

To a considerable extent the history of the world is a sor-
rowful story of men who fought and died in struggles for
liberty, the same liberty which we in this country enjoy. We
must not forget that freedom in this Nation was obtained
only through war, bloodshed, and sacrifice.

Now what is this liberty for which men have fought and
died? It is liberty of thought, liberty of speech, liberty of
conscience, liberty of action, liberty, as the Supreme Court
of the United States says, "of all the faculties". Men wanted
the right to form their own opinions and to express them in
speech or in writing. They wished to worship God according
to the dictates of their own consciences, and not as directed
by the ruler of the government. They wanted to work in
employments of their own choice, to have their own earnings
for themselves and their families, instead of having it taken
as tithes or taxes to buy purple robes for some monarch upon
a throne. They wanted the right to own property, to own a
home; and they hoped and prayed for the day when their
children might have a chance to advance in life according
to their merits. They hoped some day to have the door of
opportunity open to the son of the poor man as well as the
rich. They hoped to see class and privilege wiped away.[3]

These were the things that men and women throughout
the centuries struggled for, but which were never attained
in the whole history of the world, by any race or by any
nation, until America opened its doors to all the peoples
of the earth, guaranteeing to them all the blessings which
had been so long denied to the human race.

You will understand better the functions of government with relation to human liberty if you will realize that human liberty is a natural right. It comes from no man and no government. It is "God given". Men are born free. The love of freedom is in every human heart. Again recall the words of the Declaration of Independence—"all men are created equal . . . they are endowed by their Creator with certain unalienable Rights", among which is liberty.

America does not confer liberty upon the individual. America realizes that the individual possesses the right to liberty, and the whole structure of the American government is framed with the special purpose of protecting each individual in his natural liberty.[4]

Now there is no danger to the liberty of any one except from two sources—the wrong of a fellowman, or the wrong of the government, which in this country is a mere organization of men and women and children. Here we see emphasized the necessity for law in order to protect the liberty of the individual. Government is organized to protect individuals in their liberties. This protection is furnished by laws enacted by the people to protect the weak against the strong, the good against the evil; and in this country the same law applies to every individual. There are no special laws for special classes; every one is equally interested in having these laws as just and fair as possible. Liberty under law is the privilege of doing everything one wishes to do, except in so far as his acts may interfere in some way with like privileges of those who are about him in society.

Therefore always keep in mind that the great achievement of those who founded America was the establishment of a Nation where liberty would have a home. Of course liberty could not be fully established in this country until the Nation was fully established, until the Constitution was adopted, until laws were enacted; but from the adoption of the Constitution to the present time the people have enacted laws from time to time, and still enact laws, the better to protect every man in his liberty and to enlarge his opportunities in life.

Now in order to understand clearly how the liberties of the people are protected through our government, we must understand the nature and form of our government; and this subject we must take up at our next meeting.

NOTES AND COMMENTS

1. When Jefferson wrote "all men are created equal", he did not mean that all infant children have equal capacities for learning or accomplishment, but that all children ought to be given equal opportunities by the government of a republic. He meant that in a republic all children, whether rich or poor, whether of the aristocracy or of the common people, had great opportunities to be good and great men and women. He meant that a poor boy born in the Kentucky mountains and a rail splitter in the woods of Illinois had the opportunity to become President of the United States.

"The Declaration of Independence was not a mere temporary expedient, but is an enunciation of fundamental truths intended for all time."—William J. Bryan.

"Fourscore and seven years ago our fathers brought forth upon this continent a new nation, *conceived in liberty*, and dedicated to the proposition that all men are created equal."—Abraham Lincoln.

"Where slavery is, there *liberty* cannot be and where *liberty* is, slavery cannot be."—Abraham Lincoln.

"Respect for its (the government's) authority, compliance with its laws, acquiesence in its measures, are duties enjoined by the fundamental maxims of true Liberty."—George Washington.

"Liberty—on its positive side, denotes the fulness of individual existence; on its negative side it denotes the necessary restraint on all, which is needed to promote the greatest possible amount of liberty for each."—Bouvier's *Law Dictionary*, Vol. I, p. 217.

2. "Other nations have received their laws from conquerors; some are indebted for a constitution to the sufferings of their ancestors through revolving centuries. The people of this country, alone have formally and deliberately chosen a government for themselves, and with open and uninfluenced consent bound themselves into a social compact. Here no man proclaims his birth or wealth as a title to honorable distinction, or to sanctify ignorance and vice with the name of hereditary authority."—John Adams.

3. "Liberty means freedom in the enjoyment of all one's faculties in all lawful ways, the liberty to earn a livelihood by any lawful calling, the liberty to live and work where one wills."—*Allgeyer vs. Louisiana*, 165 *U. S.* 578.

4. "Civil liberty is the liberty belonging to men in organized society. It is liberty defined, regulated and protected by positive law of the State or recognized as existing under customary law."—*Cyclopedia of American Government*, Vol. II, p. 347.

The American people are a peculiar people. They are peculiar in their origin, peculiar in their make-up, and due to their sufferings, their persecutions, and their enduring perseverance, they are still a peculiar people. From the first white man to steer his little wooden ship westward across the great Atlantic ocean to the latest arrival among the most recent immigrants, the people coming to America have been different from those people remaining in their European homes. The conditions surrounding the lives of those people in Europe who left their homes and first settled in America were not materially different from the conditions surrounding the lives of thousands of other people who were satisfied and content to remain on their European shores. Many men thought the earth was round long before Christopher Columbus sailed away from that little seaport town in Spain to test his own ideas of finding a shorter route to India. Many people believed in religious liberty long before the Pilgrims and Puritans landed on the bleak New England shores and suffered the hardships of first settlers in a new country in order to worship God as they pleased. Many people seriously and intelligently doubted the divine right of kings, and believed in the rights of the people to govern themselves long before the American colonists adopted the Declaration of Independence. But it was left for these people—these coming Americans—to demonstrate to all the world that America was to be peopled by men and women of different ideals, different hopes, and different ambitions from all the other nations of the world.

ELEMENTARY QUESTIONS

1. What is your idea of the right to "life"? Does it mean that no one shall ever be sentenced to death for murder?
2. What is your idea of the right to "property"? Does this mean that everyone shall be wealthy? Does it mean that everyone shall own his own home?
3. What is your idea of the right to "pursuit of happiness"? Does this mean that everyone can do as he pleases?
4. Why does the judge say that liberty is the most valuable thing in the world? What would you trade for it?
5. Note the dangers to liberty that the judge points out. What are they?
6. Give an illustration of each of these dangers.
7. How may we protect ourselves against these dangers?
8. Where does this liberty that we enjoy come from? Who grants it?

ADVANCED QUESTIONS

A. In what particular ways does the Constitution of the United States guarantee liberty?
B. What forms of government existed before the United States? What liberties did the people of Russia, or France, or England enjoy in 1600?
C. Who really possesses the power of government in the United States?
D. How is the liberty of the individual protected in the United States?
E. In what ways were the people of Massachusetts in 1650 not as free as we are to-day?
F. What does it mean when we say "all men are created equal"?
G. Discuss the real meaning of the right to "Life, Liberty and the pursuit of Happiness".

H.　Write a paper on:
　　Ways in Which We Have an Equal Chance
　　How We Can Make Chances Still More Equal
　　"I hope to see the time when every American citizen will have an
　　　unfettered start and an equal chance in the race of life."—
　　　Abraham Lincoln
　　The Meaning of Liberty
　　A Week in a Land Where There Is No Liberty

IV

AMERICA—A DEMOCRACY

THE SPIRIT OF DEMOCRACY DEVELOPED UNDER THE CON-
STITUTION OF OUR COUNTRY

It is not sufficient that we shall know what government is
and where it is. We must also understand its nature. It is
the proud boast of America that it is a democracy, the first
real democracy in the world. Now what is meant by a
democracy? We hear much about democracy, and we hear
much about republicanism, and many people when they
hear or see these terms think that it has to do with the Democratic or Republican political party. We must not be confused. We must see and think clearly. Democracy and
republicanism, as we use the terms in these talks, have no
reference to any political party, but relate solely to the form
of government under which we live.

America is a democracy. It is also a republic, as we shall
see in our next talk. It is very important that we shall understand why it is a democracy, and why it is also a republic,
and the distinction between the two.

It has been well said that republicanism in government
"refers rather to the form of government", and that democracy refers to the "spirit of government". In government as
with the people the spirit is the real, important thing. In a
democracy the people govern. "A government of the people,
by the people, and for the people", as Lincoln expressed it,
is a democracy. In a democracy no man is the master of
another man without his consent. In a democracy there are
no slaves. In a democracy each and all have equal rights.
Every one in a democracy has an equal opportunity with
every other person.[1]

You have already learned that in this country the people make the laws. In the making of laws the banker and the man who digs in the sewer have the same power. Each has one vote on election day, and no more. America has no rulers except the people. In a democracy the spirit of all should be one of toleration and kindness. All of us cannot have things just as we want them in this world. Men do not all agree, so we must let the majority of the people rule. But the majority should not have any feeling of superiority. The majority should be inspired by a sense of justice and charity toward their fellowmen. In fact a democracy is a brotherhood in which each person should think, not only of himself, but of his neighbor. In this democracy the more we think of the rights of our neighbor and the more we think of our duty toward our neighbor, the better will our government be.

In a democracy we live in the belief that all men are created equal, that all through life they are equal in their rights, in their duties, and in their privileges. I do not mean of course that all men are equal in physical strength, because you who run and wrestle every day know that some are stronger than others. I do not mean that all are equal in the powers of the mind, because some of us here this morning, even some who study hard, know that other pupils get higher marks in every examination. Nor do I mean that all are equal in wealth, in health, or in comforts.

What I mean is, that so far as life and liberty are concerned, in our rights under the law, in our protection under the law, we are all equal.

In a democracy the people make the laws, and the people enforce the laws. As we shall hereafter see, every man who takes part in making a law, and every one who aids in enforcing the law is selected by the people. But the great thing about a democracy is the spirit of the people—the feeling of the people toward each other. Pride of wealth, position, race, or creed has no place in a democracy. Every person should feel sympathy and charity for his neighbor, and for his neighbor's problems in life.

We should all be willing to help those who may be less fortunate. We should all endeavor to make our neighbor's life as easy as possible.

A democracy cannot be a government by groups: it must be a government by every one.

Now I do not mean to say that we in this country all have the proper feeling toward our neighbor. We are not all good citizens of a democracy. Many people have pride, selfishness, and hate. Many people do not seem to care how the rest of the world lives. Such people are not worthy to have the privileges of living in a democracy. Many people are also ignorant in matters of government. They do not seem to care what kind of a government we have. In fact many people will not vote on election day. It is because of pride, selfishness, hate, ignorance, and indifference that I am here talking to you to-day. This is a wonderful government, but it can be made much better, with more freedom and more justice, if the people will only learn more about their power and their duty, especially if they will only cultivate the right spirit—the spirit of America, the spirit of justice, humility, kindness, and charity.

"Love thy neighbor as thyself" is not only a Christian duty, but it is the foundation of social life in a democracy. You will find when you become acquainted with life that success in life does not depend upon money, clothes, nor social position, but that in this American democracy real merit wins. More and more are we learning every day that true happiness comes only from service, service to humanity, service to our country, and this spirit of service must be developed in childhood, and expand as we grow to manhood and womanhood.

That was a nice thing you did the other day, here in this school, when you put your pennies and your nickels together, bought a ton of coal, and sent it to the widowed mother of one of your schoolmates who had been sick for several weeks. He is just a poor Polish boy; but when in health he ran errands before and after school. This helped to support his mother and his little sister. I am sure that he thinks of you every day; and that he often thanks God that his father, who died last winter, had the courage to leave the old home in Poland and come to America where there is a chance for the poorest and the most obscure.

I told you a while ago that this is the first real democracy in the world. So few people stop to think about this. The world is thousands of years old. Humanity in all these thousands of years has been made up of men, women, and children just like us. They hoped for, and dreamed of freedom, but until America became a Nation no government in the world had ever been a real government by the people. They had always been ruled by a king, a queen, an emperor, by some other ruler, by a small group of men who were rulers, or by a certain class. Your father may be a blacksmith, or a street sweeper, but on election day he can vote. Up to the organization of this government no such right existed anywhere in the world. In some countries, a few men who owned a certain amount of property could vote; but the wise men of the world sneered at the American plan to give every man the right to vote whether he owned a dollar's worth of property or not.

Always remember this, too, that even when America became a Nation, the right of all the people to vote was not granted at once. Many of our States for many years required that a voter must have a certain amount of property. Finally this was all wiped away. America has been a growth, each generation doing a little more to expand the power of the people, and this growth, this expansion must continue. We are still a young Nation and we all have much to do to aid in making this democracy a better place in which to live.

When you hear of other democracies now existing in the world, remember that America has been their guide and inspiration. Men came from France to help fight our revolution, and carried back with them the spirit of America. In time democracy was established in France. So with all the countries in the world which to-day have a greater or less degree of democracy, to them all, America has been a beacon light, a source of courage and of inspiration. Did any of you ever see the great Statue of Liberty at the entrance to the New York harbor? If you did, you saw that grand figure looking out to the east over the great expanse of water, holding aloft the great torch which in the darkness of the night is aglow with light, the great flaming torch, which is emblematic of America enlightening the world.

NOTES AND COMMENTS

1. A pure democracy would be that form of government in which *all* people of the age of twenty-one years could actually take part in making the laws and administering the government. A country would need be very small indeed, if *all* the people above twenty-one years of age could assemble in any one place and organize and conduct a meeting in which *all* could take part in law-making. No building would be large enough to accommodate all the people and even if all the people assembled out of doors, the number would be so large that those standing or sitting near the outer edge of the assembly would be so far from the speaker that they could not hear what he said when he spoke to them. A pure democracy is a physical impossibility. The nearest form of government to a pure democracy is a representative democracy, or one in which groups of people choose one or more persons to represent them. Then these representatives make laws and carry on the government in the name of *all* the people whom they represent. Therefore a democracy is that form of government in which all people have equal opportunities, and in which all may take part in the government through their chosen representatives.

"No matter how widely democracy may be extended, if it is not accompanied by a certain equality of opportunity among the members of the political society, it is not democracy."—*Cyclopedia of American Government*, Vol. I, p. 561.

"Democracy is that form of government in which the people rule. The basis of democracy is equality, as that of the aristocracy is privilege."—Bouvier's *Law Dictionary*, Vol. I, p. 540.

"The beginnings of democracy were best observed in the townships of

New England, where the Puritans from England settled and organized towns which were centers of democracy."—Peter Roberts.

In an absolute monarchy, the ruler is supreme; in a limited monarchy, the parliament or congress sets a limit to the powers of the ruler; in a democracy, the people rule.

"It is almost impossible that all the people will exactly agree on any proposition, either political or social. Therefore the rule of government in a democracy is, that *all* the people shall accept and obey those laws and regulations that are pleasing to the majority."

"The basis of our political system is the right of the *people* to make or alter their constitution of government."—George Washington.

"No man is good enough to govern another man without that other man's consent."—Abraham Lincoln.

"This country, with all its institutions, belongs to the people who inhabit it."—Abraham Lincoln.

"I believe that the American people accept, as one just definition of democracy, Napoleon's phrase, 'Every career is open to talent'."—Charles William Eliot.

Lincoln defined a democracy as "A government of the people, by the people, and for the people".

ELEMENTARY QUESTIONS

1. Which was the first real democracy to be established in the world?
2. What is a democracy? What is the difference between "democracy" and a "Democrat"?
3. Who governs in a democracy?
4. In a democracy, who makes the laws?
5. How is power in government expressed in a democracy? In America, does one man have more power than another?
6. How many times can a person vote on election day?
7. Suppose Congress or the legislature in our State passes a law that we do not like. Do we have to obey it? What can we do about it? How can we secure a change in the law?

ADVANCED QUESTIONS

A. What does "government of the people, by the people, and for the people" mean?
B. What is the proper spirit of people who live in a democracy?
C. What is meant by "the majority of the people rule"?
D. What would happen if the minority should rule? Lincoln said that this meant anarchy. Why?
E. Does the minority have any rights? Should the majority pay any attention to them? Why or why not?
F. Who enforces laws in a democracy?
G. Why is it said that the best way to get rid of a bad law is rigidly to enforce it?
H. What is the result of not casting your ballot on election day?
I. It is a fact that from election to election there is an increasing percentage of the qualified voters who do not vote. What is the danger of this? What is it likely to lead to?
J. Write a paper on:
    The Meaning of Democracy
    The Danger of Not Voting
    Why It Is Right that Women Should Vote
    Why We Fought to Make the World Safe for Democracy

V

AMERICA—A REPUBLIC

A REPRESENTATIVE FORM OF GOVERNMENT UNDER THE CONSTITUTION

As I stated to you in our last discourse, America is a democracy, but it is also a republic. It is a democracy in its spirit and the power of its people, but in the mode of exercise of the power of the people it is a republic. We often hear America referred to as a "representative democracy". If America were merely a democracy there would be no fixed method for expressing the wishes or the power of the people. In a pure democracy, people having full power would naturally assemble from time to time to decide by the vote of all those present what should be done for the public good.

You will hear of the "town meeting" which even to-day in some parts of New England is held from time to time, where the people assemble, and by vote decide matters of public concern.

But this is now a Nation of more than one hundred and five million people. We have forty-eight States, many of them very populous. When the Constitution was adopted, there were only about 3,900,000 people in all the States; but those who framed the Constitution looked into the future and could see something of the wonderful growth of the Nation which they were planning. Of course it is easy for anyone to see that in a large country like this, with a large population or a population as large as it was at the time when the Constitution was adopted, it would be impossible for all the people to assemble in a meeting to vote directly upon the passage of necessary laws, or to provide for taxation, or to conduct the general business of the State or the Nation. You can see how absolutely impossible it would be in these days to have the people of the United States assemble at the National capital to vote on any law, or to make any appropriation, or to provide rules for exercise of governmental power.

Therefore you can readily see that the founders of this country very wisely realized that the only government possible would be what is known as a representative government, a democracy where the people would have all the power, but a republic wherein the people would express that power, not directly, but through representatives or agents chosen by them.[1]

The government of the United States and that of each of the States is sub-divided into three parts: the executive, represented by the President or the Governor, the legislative, represented by Congress or the legislature, and the judicial, represented by the courts.

Now the President and the members of Congress, including the Senate, and the judges of the courts are all merely representatives of the people chosen by the people to carry out the will of the people. The position and powers of all of these representatives of the people are fixed and defined by laws enacted by the people.

As we shall hereafter find, the first law of the Nation, the foundation of all laws of the Nation, is the Constitution of the United States, which in the long ago was adopted by the people of thirteen small States.

Our form of government therefore is representative. That is to say, the people choose their representatives to do the business of the country for the people. Laws are voted for directly by members of Congress and the Senate of the United States, or members of the legislatures of the States; but these members of Congress, Senators, and legislators are selected by the people, and in voting for laws they are expressing the will of the people who voted for them. They are elected for a short term of years, so that in case any one of them should not, in his vote upon any law, carry out the wishes of the people who elected him, they may at the next election select someone else in his place who will better represent them.[2]

The important thing to bear in mind in relation to this government organization, with all the officers now necessary to do the business of the people of this great country, is that these officers—executive, legislative, and judicial—are not the government; the government rests with the people, and these officers are merely servants of the people, subject to the will of the people.

It has been well said that government in a democracy is organized public opinion. Public officers, representatives of the people, have only the power which the people give to them. In many of the States of this country, in the enactment of laws, the people by law make provision by which the people themselves have the power to reject laws enacted by their representatives of which they do not approve. Under the "initiative" and "referendum" in some States, the people retain the power to direct their legislature to enact certain laws. Also laws made by the legislature may be voted upon by the people for final approval, if desired.[3]

The important thing first to be learned is that in this democracy the government is in form a republic, because the laws are enacted and enforced, not by the direct vote of the people, but by the representatives elected by the people.

The power of the people always continues. A law may be passed by one legislature, or one session of Congress, and may be repealed the next. Any law upon the statute books may be changed from time to time, in response to the changing sentiment of the people.

We are inclined to consider the term "representative government" as relating particularly to the enactment of laws, but this is a representative government not only in the making of laws, but also in the enforcement of laws. I want you to realize early in life that every citizen has a responsibility for enforcing laws as well as for making laws, and that for any failure or omission in the making of laws, or in the enforcement of laws, the people must bear the responsibility.

NOTES AND COMMENTS

1.   "A Republic may be defined as a state in which the sovereign power rests in the people as a whole but is exercised by representatives chosen by a popular vote."—*Cyclopedia of American Government*, Vol. III, p. 188.

"A Republic, in the modern sense of the term, is a government which derives all its powers directly, or indirectly, from the great body of the people, i. e. the majority—and is administered by persons holding their offices for a limited period."—*Cyclopedia of American Government*, Vol. III, p. 188.

"Republican government is a government of the people; a government by representatives chosen by the people."—Bouvier's *Law Dictionary*.

The Constitution of the United States in Art. IV, Sec. 4 guarantees to every State a republican form of government, but it does not define what is republican government. It is generally assumed that if for any reason the representative government of a State should be destroyed or temporarily set aside, it would be the duty of the Federal government, acting through the President as chief executive, to use whatever force was necessary (including the army and navy) to overcome such agency and to restore to the people of that State its former representative government.

"It is left to Congress to decide what constitutes a republican form of government, and Congress also has the right to say which government in a state is the legal government. This necessarily follows because before Congress can decide whether the government is Republican it must decide which government is in force."—*Luther vs. Borden, 7 Howard* 1.

"It is Congress and not the President who decides what is Republican government in a state."—*Martin vs. Mott, 12 Wheaton* 19.

2.   "It may well be contended that a republican form of government necessarily involves the exercise of powers of government by representative officers and bodies, and the distribution of powers of government among distinct and independent departments."—McClain's *Constitutional Law*, p. 10.

3.   *Initiative* means the right of the people to initiate or commence the process of lawmaking. It is done by circulating a petition asking that a certain provision be enacted into law. If the petition receives the signatures of a certain percentage of qualified voters, the legislature is required to enact the provision into law, or submit it to the voters to determine whether it shall become law.

Referendum means that the qualified voters through the process of balloting may determine whether a measure proposed either through the action of the legislature, or through the initiative, shall become law.

Recall is the method by which the qualified voters may remove an undesirable officer from office before the expiration of his term. It is done through a petition requiring a certain percentage of signers from among the qualified voters. If the petition is sufficient an election is called at which time the officer may appear for continuation in office and others may appear as candidates for that office. The one receiving the largest vote is duly chosen.

ELEMENTARY QUESTIONS

1. In what respect is America a republic?
2. What is the difference between a republic and a Republican?
3. What was the population of America when the Constitution was adopted?
4. Why was it impossible to have all the people assemble to adopt laws?
5. What is meant by a representative of the people?
6. Suppose a representative does not represent the people as they wish. What can they do about it? Give illustrations.
7. Into what parts is the government of the United States divided?
8. How are the powers and duties of representatives of the people defined? Why does the judge say that the people really have the power and that this power continues?

ADVANCED QUESTIONS

A. What is the fundamental law of the United States? Why is it fundamental?
B. How can we say that the people have power in lawmaking, when we know that the representatives make the laws?
C. How can we influence the votes of our representatives?
D. If you know that your representative is likely to vote against your own wishes, what can you do about it?
E. How soon may a law be changed after it has been passed?
F. What is meant by "initiative, referendum, and recall"? How have they worked out in practice?
G. Write a paper on the following:
   The Difference between a Democracy and a Republic
   How the Public Can Make Their Representatives Represent Them
   Why America Could Not Do Without Representatives
   The New England Town Meeting

VI

LAW

NECESSITY FOR RULES OF HUMAN CONDUCT FOR GUID-ANCE AND RESTRAINT

This morning I wish to talk with you about one of the most important subjects in the world, the law; and strange to say, most people know very little about it.

Indeed I find that the average person feels that he does not need any knowledge of the law, that the law is for lawyers, judges, and courts.

Now the truth is, that there is scarcely any activity in life in which the law does not play an important part. This is true from childhood to old age, in every calling and every occupation in life.[1] The law is not intended for any one class of people, but it applies to all classes of people, the rich and the poor, the wise and the ignorant. It also applies to all ages, to men, women, and children.

What is the law, or what is a law?[2] There is nothing difficult about it. A law is merely a rule of human conduct, a rule of conduct for human beings which is enforced by the Nation, the State, or the city. There are other rules of human conduct enforced by the parents, teachers, or employers—those who have authority over others, those whose duty it is to direct the conduct of others.

Every boy knows that in his home his parents have certain rules, not written or printed, but stated by his father or mother with relation to his conduct about the home, about his school, or about his play time or vacation, when he must go to bed, when he must arise, and with whom he may associate, that he must not go in swimming unless accompanied by his father, that he shall not go to the movies without the consent of his mother, that he must attend Sunday school regularly, that he must not eat with his knife, that he must be courteous to all persons, especially the aged, that he must not play ball in the street, and a large number of other rules and directions, all intended for the good of the boy.

Then in school you find certain rules of conduct made by the Board of Education or other officers, or adopted by the teacher.

If a boy works in a store, he finds that his employer has certain rules: the time when the store shall be opened and closed; that the boy shall sweep the floor at certain hours; that he may go to lunch at a certain time; that he shall not permit other boys to pass behind the counters, etc. All of these are illustrations of rules of conduct for children, or those under the control, authority, or direction of some older person.

But older persons, the parents, the school officers, the teachers, the storekeepers, and those of all other occupations are likewise subject to rules, are under control and direction of the Nation, the State, and the city, all having power to enforce rules of conduct, called laws, which apply to the old and the young. Without such rules, such laws, it would be impossible to maintain peace and order. Without such rules, called laws, it would be impossible to protect the weak against the strong and the wicked.

This government being organized for the purpose of protecting the rights and liberties of the people, it is necessary that laws be enacted in order that our rights and liberties shall not be taken away from us by those who may be stronger or wiser than we are. Many laws prohibit wrongful acts and provide a punishment for those who commit such wrongful acts. Thus one who strikes you without justification, one who steals your bicycle, or any other property, one who breaks into your home, or into the store, a burglar, is punished. One who kills another human being, a murderer, is punished. A person who willfully sets fire to a building, or is guilty of cruelty to animals, malicious mischief, or sells liquor is punished.[3] So there are scores of different offenses forbidden by the law, and punishments fixed for those who will not obey.

There are also laws requiring that one shall ride or drive on the right hand side of the street when passing another coming from the opposite direction.

There is generally in every city a law which punishes a person who rides his bicycle upon the sidewalk. There are laws regulating the speed of automobiles, the lights and signals, and the turning at the corners of the street, so that other people either walking, or riding on bicycles, or in automobiles or other vehicles, may not receive injury.[4]

You know in this country, where every person is equal before the law, no one person has any more right in the street than his neighbor has, and the conduct of each in the use of streets and sidewalks and other public places must be such that all may enjoy equal opportunities in the use thereof.[5]

Freedom, as already explained, does not mean a right to do everything we wish to do. Freedom is the right to do whatever we may wish to do, provided it does not interfere with the right of our neighbors to have the same privileges which we claim for ourselves.

Therefore, it is absolutely necessary to have laws fixing the conduct of all persons; and it is necessary, in order to enforce these laws, to punish those who will not obey them.

Who makes these laws? In America the laws are made by the people themselves; that is, they elect representatives to serve in Congress, in the legislatures of the States, and in the councils of the city, who make the laws for the people according to the wishes of the people. This you will understand more fully as you study this representative form of government we have in this country.

The people have the right to change any law now in existence, and may also make such new laws as they think will better protect the people in their rights.[6]

Who enforces these laws, these rules of conduct? The rules of the home are enforced by the parents. If you violate the rules of your parents, they impose a punishment upon you. This punishment may not be severe, in fact it should not be, unless your disobedience is continued and stubborn.

If you violate the rules of school, the teacher or other school officers have the right to punish; and if you violate the rules of your employer, he has the right to admonish you, and of course if you do not obey, he will discharge you and you will lose your place.

Now the rules of conduct, the laws of the Nation, the State, or the city are enforced in this country by the people, through their government, through the courts, presided over by judges whom the people themselves select for that purpose. Sometimes the punishment is severe, sometimes mild. It all depends upon the character of the person who disobeys the law, and whether the disobedience is stubborn or willful. Penalties are imposed, not only to punish the wrongdoer, but as a warning to others, that if they disobey the law, they too will be punished.

In this country all laws imposing punishment for offenses are printed so that every one may know what the law is; but it is not necessary that one should study each separate law, because as a rule, your conscience will be your guide against wrong doing. There are not many acts punished by the State or Nation which are not morally wrong. The person whose heart is right knows good from evil; and the person who really tries to do right will seldom be guilty of violating any law.

I do not expect you to learn all about the different laws. This is not necessary. But I do expect you to understand enough about the law to realize that we are all subject to authority; that laws are enacted by the authority of the people; that laws are absolutely necessary, and that without laws we should have no liberty. Above all, I want you to learn that in this country the people make the laws, and I want you to feel absolute confidence in the power of the people to make and enforce laws.

I hope that you will acquire a spirit of confidence and faith in the justice of the law, and learn that submission to the law is absolutely essential in a government of the people and by the people.[7]

But there are many laws, many rules of conduct, besides those defining crimes, offenses, and the punishment of wrongdoers.

I want to talk to you briefly about some of the laws which affect our conduct in every day life, in matters not criminal. I want to impress upon you how far reaching the law is as affecting every human being in his daily conduct.[8]

Suppose one of the girls here goes to the store to buy a piece of cloth. How does she tell the merchant how much cloth she wants? She, without doubt, will say that she wants one yard, or two yards, or three yards, according to her needs. Now how much is a yard? Of course you all know that a yard is three feet. I suppose you all know that a yard is the same length in every city in the United States. We go into the store and ask for a yard of cloth in any city in the country, with absolute confidence that we will get for each yard, three feet in length. But how do we know we will get three feet in length for each yard? How do we know what we will get when we ask for a pound of coffee, or for a ton of coal, or for a quart of milk?

These weights and measures are nearly all fixed by law. When you come to read the Constitution of the United States, you will find that there is conferred upon the United States government the power to *"fix the standard of Weights and Measures".*[9]

The Constitution is the fundamental law of the land. This confers upon the United States government the right to fix all standards of measurements and all weights and measures of every kind. The United States government has this power. It is not required to exercise the power, but it has the power.

The United States government has a National Bureau of Standards,[10] which supervises weights and measurements, which coöperates with the States, and maintains uniformity, so that in every State, with reference to most things bought and sold, the law fixes definitely the quantity or dimensions. Without such laws you can see what a mass of confusion the people would be in at all times.

Severe penalties are imposed by law upon those who give short measure, or short weight,[11] in order to protect buyers against those who might defraud them.

So you see how necessary law is to the simple transactions of life, and how we are constantly relying upon the law in our daily transactions, to protect us against wrongdoers.[12]

Then again, how do you know how much the silver dollar which you are saving for Christmas is really worth? How do you know that one dollar is as valuable as another dollar? How do you know that the paper dollar which is in circulation is as valuable as the silver dollar? Well, here again when you read the Constitution of the United States, you will find that the people, when they adopted the Constitution, gave to the Congress of the United States the power:

"To coin Money, regulate the Value thereof, and of foreign Coin".[13]

Congress, with this power, has enacted numerous laws with reference to the coinage of silver and gold money, the printing of paper money, and fixing the value of such money. How helpless the people would be without such laws.

Then how do you know that the dollar you received in change at the grocery store is a real dollar? There are many counterfeit dollars made by wrongdoers, by criminals who seek to profit by manufacturing money themselves, sometimes so much like the genuine, that it is almost impossible to detect the difference. There are counterfeit bills, and counterfeit coin, which I dare say could not be distinguished from the genuine by any person in this room. But there are laws enacted by Congress providing very severe punishment for any person who makes, passes, or attempts to pass, any counterfeit coin. For instance, if one shall make, or pass, or attempt to pass counterfeit gold or silver coin, he may be punished by five years imprisonment in the penitentiary.[14] Even for making, or passing, or attempting to pass a one cent, two cent, three cent, or five cent piece, a person may be imprisoned for five years.[15] Any one who makes a die or mold designed for the coining, or making of counterfeit coins may be punished by imprisonment in the penitentiary for ten years.[16]

These are severe penalties. Liberty is dear, and yet you can see how absolutely necessary it is to have these severe penalties in order to protect you, your father and mother, and all other persons from being defrauded and wronged by the use of counterfeit money which is worthless, but which most people cannot distinguish from the genuine.

I suppose you watched for the letter carrier this morning. Perhaps you were expecting a letter from a friend or relative. The letter carrier came to your door. You did not have to walk to the post office. Perhaps your friend lives one thousand miles away. How is it possible for you to receive a letter in perhaps a couple of days from that far distant point? Did you ever stop to think about it? Of course you say, "Well it came through the post office". Yes, but the postoffice is only a part of the great postal system of this country, which carries your letters from one end of the land to another for the small amount of two cents; and we have wonderful confidence in this postal service. **We** carelessly drop into the mail box most important letters, often most sacred, but we have no doubt that the letter will reach its destination safely.[17]

How is it all possible? Well, again, in reading the Constitution you will find that the people gave to Congress the power:

"To establish Post Offices and Post roads".[18]

This power has been exercised by the enactment of many laws by Congress providing for post offices, letter carriers, postal clerks, railway mail service, rural routes, and many laws severely punishing any one in the postal service who willfully fails to perform his duties.

Persons engaged in the postal service may be sent to the penitentiary for stealing money from the mails, stealing a letter from the mails, for any act of dishonesty, or failure of prescribed duty. How could the great postal service of this country be maintained without such laws? How would the people have the blessing of a great service of this kind without the most carefully prepared laws made to protect the people?

So I might go on giving numerous other illustrations of the laws enacted by the people through their representatives, for the benefit of the people themselves, for their comfort, their convenience, and their protection against wrongdoers, who might deprive them of their property, or of things still more sacred than property.

I have only used these illustrations to impress upon you the great truth that there is hardly any relation in life in which the law does not have an important part. We should realize early in life that law is absolutely necessary to guide human conduct, to restrain wrongful conduct, to punish wrong doing, and thus to aid in protecting us in our right to life, liberty, and property.

These laws are not the judges' laws, nor the lawyers' laws;

they are the laws of the people, made for their benefit, worthy of our most earnest support, calling upon us for loyal obedience, demanding our respect, and inspiring our confidence.

NOTES AND COMMENTS

1. Children who attend the public school are subject to the law as well as are grown people who work in factories or on farms. The teacher must have rules and regulations governing the conduct of pupils in school. These are laws which the children must obey. If a pupil insists on disturbing other pupils or talking out loud—such may be a violation of the rules governing a good school and the pupil may be punished for such violation.

2. Law has been defined as: "The aggregate of those laws and principles of conduct which the governing power in a community recognizes as the rules and principles which it will enforce or sanction, and according to which it will regulate, limit, or protect the conduct of its members."—Bouvier's *Law Dictionary*, Vol. II, p. 144.

"Law consists of the rules and methods by which society compels or restrains the actions of its members."

In the legal sense—A law is a rule which the courts will enforce. The courts will not enforce all rules, and therefore there are many rules which are not law in the legal sense.

"Law *might* be defined as the aggregate of those rules and principles promulgated by legislative authority or established by local custom, and our laws are the resultant derived from a combination of the divine or moral laws, the laws of nature and human experience, as such resultant has been evolved by human intellect, influenced by the virtue of the ages."—*Words and Phrases*, p. 33.

"Law has her seat in the bosom of God; her voice in the harmony of the world."—Hooker.

"Laws are the very bulwark of liberty. They define every man's rights, and stand between and defend individual liberties of all."—J. G. Holland.

"Laws exist in vain for those who do not have the courage and the means to defend them."—Thomas B. Macauley.

"Laws, written, if not on stone tablets, yet on the azure of infinitude, in the inner heart of God's creation, certain as life, certain as death, are they, and thou shalt not disobey them."—Thomas Carlyle.

"A rule of civil conduct prescribed by the supreme power in a state."—Bouvier's *Law Dictionary*.

3. Laws and rules are statements of what has been agreed upon as proper conduct among persons who associate together. A person living on a lonely island in the ocean with no other person near would not need law. But as soon as two persons share the island and its fruits and animals and plants, then certain rules need be set up for the protection of each against the other. Where people are most closely associated, we need the greatest number of rules or laws. People living in large cities must more often heed law than do those living in rural districts.

4. A person may drive an automobile at twenty miles per hour on a country road with perfect safety, but twenty miles per hour in a crowded city would be positively dangerous to people crossing the streets. Therefore the speed limit of five or perhaps ten miles per hour in cities.

5. People have as much right to walk on the sidewalks of the town or city as do other people to drive teams and wagons or automobiles on

the streets. Each must obey the traffic laws. At crossings their rights of passage conflict, therefore each must be on the look-out when crossing the street. The law provides street crossings, therefore footmen must not "cut the crossings" but go the directed way.

6. When election time comes each year, or every two years, those who are qualified to vote ought by all means give careful consideration to the candidates for office and to the issues that constitute the campaign. It requires good men to make good laws. Good men are only chosen to office when good people interest themselves in the candidates and attend the elections and cast intelligent votes. Good laws are properly enforced only when good men are chosen to office.

7. "A child, an apprentice, a pupil, a mariner, and a soldier owe respectively obedience to the lawful commands of the parent, the master, the teacher, the captain of the ship, and the military officer having command; and in case of disobedience submission may be enforced by correction."—Bouvier's *Law Dictionary*, Vol. II, p. 531.

"To obey is better than sacrifice."

"Children, obey your parents in all things; for this is well pleasing unto the Lord."

"Servants, obey in all things your masters according to the flesh; not with eye service, as men pleasers; but in singleness of heart, fearing God."

"Masters, give unto your servants that which is just and equal; knowing that ye also must be obedient."—Quotations from *The Bible*.

"The capacity of the people for self government, and their willingness, ... to submit to all needful restraints, and exactions of municipal law, have been favorably exemplified in the history of the American States."—Martin Van Buren.

"Let us have faith that right makes might and in that faith let us to the end dare do our duty as we understand it."—Abraham Lincoln.

"Surely I do not misinterpret the spirit of the occasion when I assume that the whole body of the people convenant with me today to support and defend the Constitution and . . . . to yield a willing obedience to all the laws, and each to every other citizen his equal civil and political liberty."—Benj. Harrison.

"Patriotism calls for the faithful performance of all the duties of citizenship in small matters as well as great, at home as well as on tented fields."—William J. Bryan.

8. We must see ourselves as we are, moving in our daily life, guarded and safeguarded in every act by law. Every act in life is lawful or unlawful; that is, we are protected by the law in our every act, or we are condemned or punished. Here are two children on their way to school, one walking upon the sidewalk, exercising a lawful right; one riding his bicycle upon the sidewalk, performing an unlawful act. The one is an example of a careful law-abiding citizen, the other an example of a law-violator.

9. Constitution of the United States, Art. I, Sec. 8, Cl. 5.

10. Created by an Act of Congress of March 3rd, 1901. It is a bureau of the Department of Commerce, and is charged with comparing the standards used in scientific investigations, commerce, and educational institutions with standards adopted and recognized by the government.

11. 12. The Thirty-fifth General Assembly of the State of Iowa provided for a State Inspector of Weights and Measures whose duty is to travel over the State and investigate conditions among those who buy and sell, and to make arrests and prosecute those found defrauding others

by giving short weights or measures, or who sell or offer for sale spoiled foods, or keep their shops or stores in an unsanitary condition.

13. Constitution of the United States, Art. I, Sec. 8, Cl. 5.

14. 15. 16. *Revised Statutes of the United States*, Sec. 5413 and following.

17. Very few letters are ever lost in the mails. The writer one time addressed a letter to a friend living in Sydney, Australia. It was mailed at Iowa City, Iowa, and was sent east. That letter went by way of New York, England, France, Italy, the Suez Canal, and the Indian Ocean to Sydney, Australia. The person to whom it was sent had, in the meantime, left Sydney and the letter failed of delivery. About three months after being first mailed it was returned to the writer whose return address was on the outside of the envelope. In being returned it came by way of the Pacific Ocean to San Francisco and across the United States from the west. The letter had encircled the globe and was returned safely to the original sender. Pretty good work for the International Mail System.

18. Constitution of the United States, Art. I, Sec. 8, Cl. 7.

ELEMENTARY QUESTIONS.

1. What is a law?
2. By whom is a law enforced?
3. Name an activity in life that the law has nothing to do with.
4. Make a list of some of the laws that your father and mother make in your home.
5. Make a list of some of the rules of conduct found in school.
6. Go to a store in your town. Are there rules of conduct for the clerks? What are they?
7. Who makes the rules in a home? In a school? In business institutions?
8. Upon which side of the street must a person drive? Why?
9. Who fixes the rules of measurement and weight?
10. Suppose that you buy a ton of coal and find later on that you only received 1500 pounds. Could you do anything about it? Why should the coal dealer be punished?
11. What would it be like if we had no laws at all?

ADVANCED QUESTIONS

A. In imposing punishment upon a wrongdoer, what elements does the judge consider in fixing the amount of fine or the length of punishment?
B. Why do we have our laws printed? What would be the dangers of having secret laws concerning the nature and existence of which the people could not obtain information?
C. What is the distinction between a rule of conduct in the home and a law of the land?
D. List a number of laws and penalties in addition to those cited by the judge.
E. Why cannot one have liberty without law?
F. Why are people punished when they break the law?
G. Is it ever right to break the law?
H. Write a paper on the following:
   Why Breaking the Postal Laws Deserves Severe Punishment
   Liberty Under the Law
   The Danger of Counterfeit Money
   Laws that Should Be Passed
   How to Have a Law Passed

VII

THE CONSTITUTION

We now take up the subject of the Constitution of the United States. It is important because it is the foundation of the rights and liberties of all Americans. It relates to the rights and liberties of everyone in this room. It is our great charter.

Gladstone, the great English statesman, once said, "It is the greatest work ever struck off at any one time by the mind and purpose of man."[1] It is quite a long document. I want every one of us to read it carefully and study it thoroughly.

The larger part of the Constitution consists of provisions telling of the qualifications and manner of election of the President, Senators, and congressmen, the powers and duties of the various parts of our government, procedure of government, and the relations of the Nation and the States. These are important.

But more important still are the ways in which the Constitution guarantees the rights, liberties, and privileges of all men, women, and children who live under the American flag. These guaranties are numerous, but they are briefly stated. Any of us can understand them if we but read them carefully and catch their meaning. It ought not to be difficult to cause a person to study the things which relate to himself, to the most important things in his own life. Liberty we prize most dearly. Everyone of these guaranties in the Constitution is intended to guard and protect the freedom and liberty which you and I enjoy.[2]

To make our task more simple, I have selected from the

Constitution those sections which deal with our privileges as American citizens. You can see them in the copy of the Constitution which you have. (See page 217.) I have grouped these together and for convenience I shall call it "The Short Constitution". As you can see, there is nothing in it that is not in the original Constitution. It is just as if I had taken a pair of shears, cut out these phrases from the Constitution, and pasted them together. It makes it more convenient for us.

Take this "Short Constitution" home with you. Bring it with you when you come to school. Talk with your father and mother about it. It may be that sometime a knowledge of these rights that every American citizen now has may save to you your home, your freedom, or your life.

Now I am going to read this:

THE SHORT CONSTITUTION

Article I (*Amendment I.*)

Congress shall make no law respecting an establishment of religion, or prohibiting the free exercise thereof; or abridging the freedom of speech, or of the press; or the right of the people peaceably to assemble, and to petition the Government for a redress of grievances.

Article II (*Amendment II.*)

A well regulated Militia, being necessary to the security of a free State, the right of the people to keep and bear Arms, shall not be infringed.

Article III (*Amendment III.*)

No Soldier shall, in time of peace, be quartered in any house, without the consent of the Owner, nor in time of war, but in a manner to be prescribed by law.

Article IV (*Amendment IV.*)

The right of the people to be secure in their persons, houses, papers, and effects, against unreasonable searches and seizures, shall not be violated, and no Warrants shall issue, but upon probable cause, supported by Oath or affirmation, and particularly describing the place to be searched, and the persons or things to be seized.

Article V (*Amendment V.*)

No person shall be held to answer for a capital, or otherwise infamous crime, unless on a presentment or indictment of a Grand Jury, except in cases arising in the land or naval forces, or in the Militia, when in actual service in time of War or public danger; nor shall any person be subject for the same offence to be twice put in jeopardy of life or limb; nor shall be compelled in any criminal case to be a witness against himself, nor be deprived of life, liberty, or property, without due process of law; nor shall private property be taken for public use, without just compensation.

Article VI (*Amendment VI.*)

In all criminal prosecutions, the accused shall enjoy the right to a speedy and public trial, by an impartial jury of the State and district wherein the crime shall have been committed, which district shall have been previously ascertained by law, and to be informed of the nature and cause of the accusation; to be confronted with the witnesses against him; to have compulsory process for obtaining witnesses in his favor, and to have the Assistance of Counsel for his defence.

Article VII (*Amendment VII.*)

In suits at common law, where the value in controversy shall exceed twenty dollars, the right of trial by jury shall be preserved, and no fact tried by a jury shall be otherwise re-examined in any Court of the United States, than according to the rules of the common law.

Article VIII (*Amendment VIII.*)

Excessive bail shall not be required, nor excessive fines imposed, nor cruel and unusual punishments inflicted.

Article IX (*Amendment IX.*)

The enumeration in the Constitution, of certain rights, shall not be construed to deny or disparage others retained by the people.

Article X (*Amendment X.*)

The powers not delegated to the United States by the Constitution, nor prohibited by it to the States, are reserved to the States respectively, or to the people.

Article XI (*Amendment XIII, Sec. 1.*)

Neither slavery nor involuntary servitude, except as a punishment for crime whereof the party shall have been duly convicted, shall exist within the United States, or any place subject to their jurisdiction.

Article XII (*Amendment XIV, Sec. 1.*)

All persons born or naturalized in the United States, and subject to the jurisdiction thereof, are citizens of the United States and of the State wherein they reside. No State shall make or enforce any law which shall abridge the privileges or immunities of citizens of the United States; nor shall any State deprive any person of life, liberty, or property, without due process of law; nor deny to any person within its jurisdiction the equal protection of the laws.

Article XIII (*Amendment XV, Sec. 1.*)

The right of citizens of the United States to vote shall not be denied or abridged by the United States, or by any State on account of race, color, or previous condition of servitude.

Article XIV (*Art. I, Sec. 9, Cl. 2.*)

The Privilege of the Writ of Habeas Corpus shall not be suspended, unless when in Cases of Rebellion or Invasion, the public Safety may require it.

Article XV (*Art. I, Sec. 9, Cl. 3.*)

No Bill of Attainder or ex post facto law shall be passed.

Article XVI (*Art. I, Sec. 9, Cl. 8.*)

No Title of Nobility shall be granted by the United States: And no Person holding any Office of Profit or Trust under them, shall, without the Consent of the Congress, accept of any present, Emolument, Office or Title of any kind whatever, from any King, Prince, or foreign State.

Article XVII (*Art. III, Sec. 2, Cl. 3.*)

The trial of all Crimes except in Cases of Impeachment, shall be by Jury, and such Trial shall be held in the State where the said Crimes shall have been committed; but when not committed within any State, the Trial shall be at such Place or Places as the Congress may by Law have directed.

Article XVIII (*Art. III, Sec. 3, Cl. 1.*)

Treason against the United States, shall consist only in levying War against them, or in adhering to their

Enemies, giving them Aid and Comfort. No person shall be convicted of Treason unless on the Testimony of two witnesses to the same overt Act or on Confession in open Court.

The Congress shall have power to declare the Punishment of Treason, but no Attainder of Treason shall work Corruption of Blood, or Forfeiture except during the Life of the Person attainted.

Article XIX (*Art. IV, Sec. 2, Cl. 1.*)

The Citizens of each State shall be entitled to all Privileges and Immunities of Citizens in the several States.

Article XX (*Art. VI, Cl. 3.*)

No religious Test shall ever be required as a Qualification to any Office or public Trust under the United States.

Now that is not long, is it? Yet in this brief part of the Constitution are contained provisions the most important for the common people ever written by the hand of man in all the history of the world. In some countries of the world people have some of the rights and privileges guaranteed by our Constitution, but in no other country in the world do the people have a written guaranty of all the rights, privileges, and liberties set forth in these short extracts from the Constitution of the United States.

I want you all to get fixed in your minds the date of the adoption of the original Constitution by the convention—1787.[5] That was more than a century and a quarter ago.

I want every child to understand just why the Constitution was made, how it was made, something of the men that made it, and how the people of the States approved of the Constitution before it became binding.

I also want want you to understand something of the

changes and additions made by the people since the Constitution was first adopted. I want you to understand that it is the Constitution of the people, the whole people, and I want you to know that the people can change the Constitution or make additions to it whenever they want to.[6]

So at our next meeting I am going to tell you something of the making of the Constitution.

NOTES AND COMMENTS

1. There are four general theories as to the origin of the Constitution of the United States: (1) That it was an entirely new document. This theory was inspired by the statement of Gladstone. People who heard Mr. Gladstone or read of his comment on the Constitution misinterpreted his saying and came to believe he meant that that great Constitution was the work of the moment as conceived by the men in the convention at Philadelphia. No one knew better than Mr. Gladstone himself that such was not true. (2) That it was copied almost entirely after the English constitution of that time. This was the theory of Sir Henry Maine, and it was just as erroneous as was the common acceptance of Gladstone's statement. There are many things in the Constitution of the United States that were not in the English constitution of that time. (3) That it was based entirely upon the experience of the colonists themselves. This theory is also incorrect as the facts show that many fundamentals of the Constitution were copied directly from the governments of European countries. (4) That it was due to all the above influences taken together, but that they were worked out by the colonists and the Constitution makers in their many years of experience in making Constitutions for the States after their independence from England, and during the time of the Confederation.

A careful study of the debates in the convention at Philadelphia will reveal the fact that the different governments, institutions, rulers, and statesmen of Europe were referred to in the making of the Constitution.

During the discussions in the convention one hundred and thirty allusions were made to the government and institutions of England. The allusions made to France numbered nineteen. Those made to the German States were seventeen. Those made to Holland were nineteen. Greece was referred to thirteen times; Switzerland was alluded to five times; and Rome was alluded to sixteen times.

The English government and institutions were held up as a model to be imitated fifty times; as an example to be avoided, twenty-four times. France was held up as a model three times, and as a warning five times. Rome was cited five times as a model and seven times as a warning.

From the standpoint of training, experience, and general qualifications for constitution makers, the delegates who sat in the Federal convention at Philadelphia were the most remarkable group of statesmen the world has ever seen. Sixty-five delegates were chosen, of whom fifty-five attended the convention and of these thirty-nine signed the Constitution, three were present but refused to sign, and thirteen were absent on the last day. Of the fifty-five who sat in the convention, twenty-five were from northern States and thirty from southern States. Of the thirty-nine signers, nineteen were from the North and twenty from the South.

Of the fifty-five men thirty were college men, twenty-six had degrees, forty-seven were afterwards prominent in public life; of the remaining eight, at least four died soon after the close of the convention. The most noted men were: Washington, Franklin, Hamilton, Madison, Wilson, Patterson, Gerry, Sherman, Pinckney, and Randolph. Six men who signed the Constitution had also signed the Declaration of Independence—Benjamin Franklin, James Wilson, Robert Morris, and George Clymer of Pennsylvania, Roger Sherman of Connecticut, and George Read of Delaware.—Meyerholz's *The Federal Convention.*

2. Montesquieu, a famous French writer of the eighteenth century, tells us that political liberty consists in the security one feels in doing whatever the law permits. However we must remember that the laws themselves must likewise be sound.

3. We must notice that Article I of "The Short Constitution" commences, *"Congress shall make no law"* etc., which means that these first eight amendments to the Constitution of the United States apply only to the Federal government, and are limitations on the powers of Congress rather than on the powers of the States. However most States have similar provisions in their Constitutions.

4. Article X is important because it tells in a few words the exact relation of the States to the Federal government.

5. Article V of the main body of the Constitution provides that when nine States should ratify the Constitution, it should be established as the frame of government. The first State to ratify was Delaware, December 7, 1787; the ninth State was New Hampshire, June 21, 1788; and the last State was Rhode Island, May 29, 1790.

6. George Washington expressed the vast importance of this thought when he said: *"The basis of our political system is the right of the people to make or alter their constitution of government."*

"The Constitution is itself in every rational sense and to every useful purpose a bill of rights."—Alexander Hamilton.

"Much of the strength and efficiency of any government in procuring and securing happiness to the people depends on opinion, on the general opinion of the goodness of the government, as well as of the wisdom and integrity of its governors. I hope, therefore, for our own sakes, as a part of the people and for the sake of our posterity, that we shall act heartily and unanimously in recommending this Constitution wherever our influence may extend, and turn our future thoughts and endeavors to the means of having it well administered."—Benjamin Franklin.

"In the fullness of time a Republic rose up in the wilderness of America. Thousands of years had passed away before this child of the ages could be born. From whatever there was of good in the systems of former centuries, she drew her nourishment; the wrecks of the past were her warnings. The wisdom which had passed from India through Greece, with what Greece had added of her own, the jurisprudence of Rome, the mediaeval municipalities, the Teutonic method of representation, the political experience of England, the benignant wisdom of the expositors of the law of nature and of nations in France and Holland, all shed on her their selectest influence. Out of all the discoveries of statesmen and sages, out of all the experience of past human life, she compiled a perennial political philosophy, the primordial principles of national ethics—she sought the vital elements of social forms and blended them harmoniously in the free commonwealth which comes nearest to the illustration of the natural equality of all men. She entrusted the guardianship of established rights to law; the movement of reform to the spirit of the people and drew her force from the happy reconciliation of both."—George Bancroft.

"In spite of its supposed precision, and its subjection to judicial construction, our constitution has always been indirectly made to serve the turn of that sort of legislation which its friends call progressive, and its enemies call revolutionary, quite as effectively as though Congress had the omnipotence of parliament. The theory of the latent powers to carry out those granted has been found elastic enough to satisfy almost any party demands in time of peace, to say nothing of its enormous extensions in time of war."—*The Nation*, November 7, 1872, No. 384, p. 300.

"Our fathers by an almost divine prescience, struck the golden mean." —Pomeroy's *An Introduction to the Constitutional History of the United States*, p. 102.

"It (the United States Constitution) ranks above every other written Constitution for the intrinsic excellence of its scheme, its adaptation to the circumstances of the people, the simplicity, brevity and precision of its language, its judicious mixture of definition in principle with elasticity in details. One is induced to ask, to what causes, over and above the capacity of its authors and the patient toil they bestowed upon it, these merits are due, or in other words, what were the materials at the command of the Philadelphia Convention for the achievement of so great an enterprise as the creation of a nation by means of an instrument of government. The American Constitution is no exception to the rule that everything which has power to win the obedience and respect of men must have its roots deep in the past, and that the more slowly every institution has grown, so much the more enduring it is likely to prove. There is little in this Constitution that is absolutely new. There is much that is as old as Magna Charta."—James Bryce, author of *The American Commonwealth*.

"Let reverence for the law be breathed by every mother to the lisping babe that prattles on her lap; let it be taught in schools, seminaries, and colleges; let it be written in primers, spelling books and almanacs; let it be preached from pulpits, and proclaimed in legislative halls, and enforced in courts of justice; let it become the political religion of the nation."—Abraham Lincoln.

"The Constitution, which may at first be confounded with the Federal Constitutions which have preceded it, rests in truth upon a wholly novel theory—a great discovery in modern political science. In all the Confederations which have preceded the American Constitution of 1787, the Allied States......agreed to obey the injunctions of a federal government; but they reserved to themselves the right of ordaining and enforcing the laws of the Union......" (The American government, he explains, claims directly the allegiance of every citizen, and acts upon each directly through its own courts and officers.) "This difference has produced the most momentous consequences."—Seocqueville's *Democracy in America*.

"It will be the wonder and admiration of all future generations and the model of all future constitutions."—William Pitt, after reading the Constitution of the United States.

"The Constitution of the United States is by far the most important production of its kind in human history. It created, without historic precedent, a federal-national government. It combined national strength with individual liberty in a degree so remarkable as to attract the world's admiration. Never before in the history of man had a government struck so fine a balance between liberty and union, between state rights and national sovereignty. The world had labored for ages to solve this greatest of all governmental problems, but it had labored in vain. Greece in her mad clamor for liberty had forgotten the need of the strength that union brings, and she perished. Rome fostered union, nationality, for its strength, until it became a tyrant and strangled the child liberty. It was left for our own Revolutionary fathers to strike the balance between these opposing forces to join them in a perpetual wedlock in such a way as to secure the benefits of both. They selected the best things that had been tried and proved. Hence their great success, hence the fact that 132 years after its signing, this same Constitution is still the supreme law of the land and more deeply imbedded in the American heart than ever."—Henry William Elson.

"The Constitution is not an arbitrary, unchangeable document, but can be adapted to meet new conditions whenever the people decide. It should be upheld because under its wise provisions the United States has developed into a great nation of happy and prosperous people; because it contains sacred guarantees of protection for the individual; and because it affords freedom and opportunity for every citizen, whether native-born or naturalized. American citizenship securely rests upon its firm foundation."—Henry Litchfield West.

"The Federal Constitution, the whole of it, is nothing but a code of the people's liberties, political and civil. The Constitution is not a mass of rules, but the very substance of our freedom, not obsolete; but in every part alive; more needful now than ever, and as fitted to our needs." —Stimson's *The American Constitution.*

"No other country in the world possesses the guarantees of individual liberty and inherent rights that are accorded by the Constitution of the United States."—David Jayne Hill's *The People's Government.*

"We need not view with apprehension or even regret the gradual adaptation of the Constitution to the ever-changing needs from generation to generation of the most progressive nation in the world. The Constitution is not a static institution. It is neither, on the one hand, a sandy beach, which is quickly destroyed by the erosion of the waves, nor, on the other hand, is it a Gibralter rock which wholly resists the ceaseless washing of time and circumstances. Its strength lies in its adaptability to slow and progressive change. While the necessity of change may be recognized in the non-essentials, yet the Constitution was based upon certain fundamental principles which were not thus changeable. These time should not wither nor custom stale. While the great compact apparently dealt only with very concrete and practical details of government in the very simplest language, and carefully avoided anything that savored of visionary doctrinarism, yet, behind these simply but wonderfully phrased delegations of power, was a broad and accurate political philosophy, which constitutes the true doctrine of American Government. Its principles are of eternal verity. They are founded upon the inalienable rights of man. They are not the thing of the day or temporary circumstance. If they are destroyed, then the spirit of our government is gone, even if the form survive."—James M. Beck.

"The Constitution remains the surest and safest foundation for a free government that the wit of man has yet devised."—Nicholas Murray Butler.

"I believe there is no finer form of government than the one under which we live, and that I ought to be willing to live or die, as God decrees, that it may not perish from the earth through treachery within or through assault without."—Thomas R. Marshall.

"Although not a citizen of your great country, I am heart and soul with you and your associates in the glorious fight you are making for the preservation of your peerless Constitution, which has made your country what it is, and which is today the brightest hope of mankind."— Baron Rosen, formerly Russian Ambassador to the United States of America.

"Under the American Constitution was realized the sublime conception of a nation in which every citizen lives under two complete and well-rounded systems of laws,—the state law and the federal law—each with its legislature, its executive, and its judiciary moving one within the other, noiselessly, and without friction. It was one of the longest reaches of constructive statesmanship ever known in the world. There never was anything quite like it before, and in Europe it needs much explanation even for educated statesmen who have never seen its workings. Yet to America it has become so much a matter of course that they, too, sometimes need to be told how much it signifies. *In 1787 it was the substitution of law for violence between states that were partly sovereign. In some future still grander convention we trust the same thing will be done between states that have been wholly sovereign, whereby peace may gain and violence be diminished over other lands than this which has set the example.*"—John Fiske, in 1888.

ELEMENTARY QUESTIONS

1. Compare "The Short Constitution" on pages 56-60 with the complete Constitution found at the back of the book.
2. Why were these parts selected from the entire Constitution? Is there any similarity in the various parts selected?
3. What are the most important provisions of the Constitution of the United States?
4. Do the guaranties of the Constitution protect the rights of all people living in America, or do they apply only to a few favored classes?
5. What was the date of the adoption of the original Constitution?

ADVANCED QUESTIONS

A. Why are we interested in our rights?
B. What are the dangers of talking too much about our rights?
C. Make a list of a duty to correspond with each right selected.
D. Write a paper on the following:
   The Officials Provided by the Constitution
   The American Bill of Rights

VIII

MAKING THE CONSTITUTION

HOW THE CONVENTION OF 1787 DRAFTED THE CONSTITUTION OF THE UNITED STATES

You will remember from your study of American history that when the early colonists came to this country they settled along the Atlantic coast in many separate and distinct groups. Not all had come from the same country. Most of them were English, but there were also smaller settlements of Dutch, French, Germans, and Swedes. It was not many years until the English had taken control of all the land from Maine to Georgia, but even then not all the English were alike. There were Puritans and Cavaliers, Scotch and Irish, Scotch-Irish and Quakers. They differed in their ideas of government, religion, and education.

These colonists had come for many purposes. Some had come to make their fortune. Others because of trouble at home. Most had come to be free, to worship God in the way they chose, to form their own government, to make their own laws, to govern themselves; and in the early days, they had met with success.

But as time went on, as more people came, as ships were built, and trade and commerce increased, the government of England became more and more tyrannical. The English people may not have favored this, but they did not direct the acts of their king and his officers. Taxes were placed on the colonists without their consent. They were forced to accept laws not of their own choosing. The king refused them the right to select their own judges. They could not trade where they pleased. If you will read the

Declaration of Independence you will see how their liberties were restricted.[1]

All this time the various colonies were as separate as so many distinct countries. They did not know each other. There was little travel from one to another. They were quite different. But they were alike in the fact that each wanted liberty, and that each was subject to oppression from the English king.

So from time to time we find them sending delegates to some common meeting place to discuss a plan of action. In 1754 a group met at Albany to suggest a plan of union. In 1765 England passed the Stamp Act which put a tax upon certain articles such as books, newspapers, and playing cards. A person could not sell one of these articles without pasting upon it one of these stamps, the money from which went to England as a tax. It was much like our war tax upon tooth paste, shaving soap, and playing cards. The difference was this. The colonists had never given the right to make this tax. It had been imposed upon them by England; and further, if a person were accused of selling a book or newspaper without this stamp, he could be severely punished.[2] This enraged the colonists, and in New York in the following year, there met a group of delegates from nearly all the colonies to discuss ways and means of meeting this.

Again in 1774, conditions having become worse, delegates from twelve colonies met at Philadelphia at the First Continental Congress to consider the grievances against Great Britain. The Second Continental Congress following it carried on the first years of the Revolutionary War. It drafted and adopted the Declaration of Independence. It raised and provided for the armies, and brought the States together.

But it needed a kind of constitution. So in 1777 the Articles of Confederation were drawn up and adopted by Congress and by 1781 all the States had finally adopted them. But they were inadequate. Each of the thirteen States wanted all the power in its own hands.[3]

You cannot blame them. Picture to yourself these little settlements down on the Atlantic Coast. All together they did not have as many people as there are in the State of New Jersey to-day. They and their fathers had left their homes and traveled thousands of miles over stormy seas to find liberty. They themselves had fought a long war against England to make themselves free. They did not wish to give up these powers.[4]

But the wiser people in the different States saw that to form a more perfect union it was necessary to grant the central government more powers, and to fix forever certain rights which every American citizen should enjoy throughout the years to come. So the people selected men as their representatives and authorized them to meet with the representatives from other States at Philadelphia in 1787 to draw up a plan of government which would be strong enough to hold the country together and govern it effectively.

Now who were these men? They were men who were selected by their neighbors to represent them, just as men are elected to-day to represent us in the legislature of our State or in Congress. To be sure, in those days not all men were allowed the right to vote. In some States a man had to have a certain amount of money before he could vote. In others men of certain religious faiths were not allowed to vote. But the delegates to the Constitutional Convention were men who were fairly representative of all the people. When we consider the work that they did, that they wrote our Constitution, that they were able to do this at the time they did, we must feel that a wise Providence guided their selection and inspired them in their wonderful work.

There in Independence Hall in Philadelphia were Benjamin Franklin and George Washington, James Madison and

Edmund Randolph, Alexander Hamilton and Gouverneur Morris. Almost all the prominent men of the time took part.[5]

They took the best that they knew of the experience of the human race in government, especially the experience of England and America, and from this they drew up the Constitution of the United States, the foundation of the government under which we live.[6]

When they had finished their work—that part of the Constitution which precedes the amendments—they submitted it to the States. They were very careful to see to it that the people themselves should approve of this. So instead of having the usual legislature of each State vote upon it, they provided that the people of each State should elect delegates for a special convention, the sole purpose of which was to decide whether or not they would like to live under a government like this.[7] These conventions, elected by the people for this special purpose, met and one after another, often after a bitter struggle, ratified the Constitution. The chief objection was that the rights of all Americans were not clearly stated.

So at the first meeting of Congress, the first ten amendments—our American Bill of Rights—were adopted and in 1791 they were ratified by the States. Since then the Constitution has been rarely amended. In 1798 and in 1804 the eleventh and twelfth amendments regarding the courts and the election of the President were adopted. After the Civil War three amendments were adopted regarding the problem of the negro citizen. Since then we have added changes regarding the income tax, the election of United States Senators, and prohibition. The last amendment, dealing with the extension of the vote to women, was ratified by Tennessee as the thirty-sixth State on August 18, 1920.

To-day then, our government is founded upon the Constitution made shortly after the Revolutionary War. It represents the aims and ambitions of the fathers of our country. They came to this land to be free. They suffered persecution. They threw off the yoke of the oppressor. They established a government of the people, by the people, for the people. The people selected the men who drew it up. They selected the men who amended it. Our task is to understand what it means, to obey it, and protect it.

The lofty purpose of the fathers of the republic in establishing this, the first real government by the people, is expressed in these thrilling words:

"We the people of the United States, in Order to form a more perfect Union, establish Justice, insure domestic Tranquility, provide for the common defence, promote the general Welfare, and secure the Blessings of Liberty to ourselves and our Posterity, do ordain and establish this CONSTITUTION for the United States of America."

NOTES AND COMMENTS

1. The English government forced laws upon the colonies to restrict trade and manufactures, to place a standing army in America, and to raise taxes. The tax laws were denounced as illegal by the colonists, who argued that they were not represented in Parliament.

Read the charges made against the king and the government of England in the Declaration of Independence.

2. Read the famous speech made by James Otis against the Stamp Act in the Stamp Act Congress in New York, October, 1765. See *American History Leaflets.*

3. The following were the fundamental defects of the Articles of Confederation.

a. They did not provide for a central executive, and there was no supreme executive to enforce the laws.

b. No provision was made for a central judiciary, and each State interpreted the Federal laws as it saw fit.

c. They permitted concurrent legislation on vital subjects: i. e. each State could legislate as it pleased on such subjects as tariff, foreign treaties, currency, etc.

d. They permitted each State to regulate its own coinage and there were at one time at least fourteen different kinds of coins in the thirteen States. This greatly interfered with trade.

e. They gave Congress no power to enforce the observance of treaties. Congress could pass laws but could not enforce them.

f. They gave Congress no power to coerce a State—it could only recommend to the States.

g. They required a two-thirds vote on all questions in Congress, and votes were cast by States. Most bills may pass the present Congress by a majority vote.

h. Congress could not reach the individual to punish him for crime committed against the Federal government, except through the State in which the crime was committed. Often the States refused to act.

i. The Articles could not be amended without the consent of *all* of the States. Several times one State defeated the amendment of the Articles.

4. The small States having only small areas and therefore less room for settlers, were afraid of any form of union government which gave the States proportional representation in Congress. These small States declared they would not ratify the Articles of Confederation until those States having large areas of western lands would agree to cede those lands to the Federal government. The seven States holding western lands agreed to cede their lands in January, 1781, and on March 1st, Maryland as the last State ratified the Articles of Confederation.

5. The various States chose a total of sixty-five delegates to attend the Federal convention at Philadelphia. Of these, fifty-five actually sat in the convention. Of the entire number, forty-two were present on the last day and thirty-nine signed the Constitution.

Of the fifty-five who sat in the convention, twenty-five were from north of the Mason and Dixon Line, or from the northern States, and thirty were from the southern States. Of the thirty-nine signers, nineteen were from the North and twenty from the South. The three who refused to sign were Elbridge Gerry of Massachusetts and Edmund Randolph and George Mason of Virginia. These three men thought the Constitution gave too much power to the central government and did not leave enough to the States.

Eight of the men who signed the Constitution were of foreign birth. They were Alexander Hamilton, William Patterson, James Wilson, Robert Morris, James McHenry, Thomas Fitzsimons, William R. Davie, and Pierce Butler. You will notice that Hamilton, Wilson, Patterson, and Morris were among the most influential men in the convention. Many of America's greatest men have been of foreign birth.

The oldest man in the convention was Benjamin Franklin who was eighty-one years of age. The youngest man was Jonathan Dayton of New Jersey who was only twenty-seven. Charles Pinckney was twenty-nine years old, and Alexander Hamilton was thirty. The average age of the entire membership in the convention was 43% years.

The membership in the convention included a remarkable group of men—in fact the most remarkable group of statesmen that ever assembled for the making of a constitution. They had gained their experience in five different ways: colonial legislatures, State legislatures, State conventions, Continental Congresses, and in the Congress of the Confederation. Six of them had the honor of having signed the Declaration of Independence—Benjamin Franklin, James Wilson, Robert Morris, Roger Sherman, George Read, and George Clymer. Thirty delegates were college men and twenty-six had degrees.

6. A careful study of the debates in the Federal convention will reveal the following allusions to the government and institutions of other countries. A total of two hundred and twenty-three allusions were made to the governments of Europe, the most important of which were the following: one hundred and thirty allusions were made to England, of which fifty were commendatory, and twenty-four were warnings; nineteen allusions were made to France, of which five were commendatory and three were warnings; Germany, or rather the German States, had

seventeen allusions; Holland had twenty allusions; Greece had twenty-five; Rome had twenty-six. The two hundred and twenty-three allusions were made in such way as to indicate that the delegates were widely read in both government and history.

7. The Constitution in Article VII says, "The Ratification of the Conventions of nine States shall be sufficient for the Establishment of this Constitution between the States so ratifying the Same."

The first State to ratify was Delaware on December 7, 1787. New Hampshire, the ninth State, ratified on June 21, 1788, and Rhode Island, the last, on May 29, 1790.

ELEMENTARY QUESTIONS

1. Why did the early settlers come to America?
2. From what countries did they come? Which countries were most important?
3. Why did they become dissatisfied with English rule here?
4. Why did they wish to unite? Name some of the earlier attempts at union.
5. When was the Stamp Act passed? What was it supposed to do? Why did the colonists object?
6. Why were the Articles of Confederation not satisfactory?
7. What was the meeting in Philadelphia in 1787? How were the representatives at this meeting chosen? How did they try to see that the representatives at this meeting actually represented the people?
8. How was the Constitution ratified by the people? In what way did they try to make it the actual will of the people?
9. When was our Bill of Rights passed?
10. What amendments have been added to the Constitution since 1791?

ADVANCED QUESTIONS

A. How did the makers of the Constitution guard against the abuses cited in the Declaration of Independence?
B. How were the defects in the Articles of Confederation guarded against and remedied?
C. What experience had the makers of the Constitution had which enabled them to prepare so successful a document?
D. Would you say that Gladstone's statement, "it is the greatest work ever struck off at any one time by the mind and purpose of man" was literally true?
E. How did the allusions to other countries made during the convention show the advantage of America's being a "melting pot"?
F. What people were allowed to vote at the time of the adoption of the Constitution?
G. What were the chief objections urged against ratification of the Constitution?
H. Write a paper on the following:
   Why the People Needed a Constitution
   The Main Points Included
   A Comparison of the Work Done Then and the Outline Made in Answers to Questions J Chapter Two
   George Washington
   Benjamin Franklin
   Alexander Hamilton
   James Madison

IX

FREEDOM

This morning we begin the consideration of what I believe to be the most important of all the subjects we have talked about. I think people are more interested in their privileges and rights than they are in their duties. In fact we hear a great deal and we read a great deal about "rights", but we do not find very much said on the streets, in the homes, or in the newspapers about our "duties".[1]

Now we have considered in a very general way the nature of our government and something of our powers and duties under the Constitution. I know that you will be interested in considering our rights and privileges under the Constitution of the United States.

Always keep in mind that each State has a Constitution, and that the Nation has a Constitution, that the Constitution of the United States covers the entire Nation, not only the original thirteen colonies, but the present forty-eight States, and that any States that may hereafter be brought in the Union will have as their fundamental law the Constitution adopted by the people in the long ago.[2]

Also always keep in mind that the Nation has certain powers, and that the Constitution of the United States is supreme only as to the things over which the United States as a Nation has control.

But it is important to bear in mind that the great principles of the Constitution of the United States have been carried into the Constitutions of the various States, and that the rights and privileges of the people under the Constitution of the United States have also to a large extent been guaranteed by the Constitutions of the States.[3]

This morning we take up a constitutional guaranty which you perhaps have not thought much about, but which is one of the most important in the whole Constitution—*Freedom of Worship*. The Constitution provides:

"Congress shall make no law respecting an establishment of religion, or prohibiting the free exercise thereof".[4]

As we look back through the history of the world we are startled to find that this was the first written guaranty that the people of any nation ever had permitting them to worship God according to the dictates of their own conscience.[5]

Now some of you may not realize how important this is; but there is nothing so dear to the human heart as the right, the privilege, of belonging to that church and worshipping God in that manner which each individual may desire. We do not realize the value of such a privilege until some one, or some power, seeks to take it away from us. All through the world men and women and children have fought, and many of them have died, for this privilege. It was the custom of the nations of the world before our Constitution to have an established religion, a National religion, and in many of the countries it was the law that every one must belong to the state church, and must actually believe in the religion of the state. In fact, in many countries, refusal to believe in the religion of the state was punished by death— sometimes by burning to death, and I am sure you will be surprised to realize that while America was first settled by people who were seeking religious freedom, they were still so imbued with a feeling of the old days that persons must worship, not as their conscience might dictate, but as the state might dictate, that for many years in this country in certain of the colonies a state religion was recognized, and obligation to conform to the established religion enforced by severe penalties.

In the colony of Virginia the established or state church existed, and it was the law that any person who did not conform thereto should be punished by burning to death. This is startling, isn't it, to hear of such a brutal law upon American soil? Virginia afterwards became the pioneer in legislation establishing freedom of worship, but it took the most strenuous efforts of Thomas Jefferson through many years to finally wipe out these cruel laws and establish freedom of worship.[6]

The Virginia statute granting absolute freedom of worship was the first ever adopted in the history of the world by any state or nation, the first guaranty of the right. Freedom of worship had existed before this in Maryland under the generous rule of Lord Baltimore, but the first formal statute was adopted in Virginia.

Now your teachers tell me that in this school the pupils belong to sixteen different churches. I suppose each one of you thinks that the church to which he belongs is better than any of the others. I hope you do. I hope that every child is sincere in his religious belief, whatever it may be. But how would you feel if some representative of the State should come here this morning, and announce that a law had been passed by which every pupil must belong to the Baptist, the Methodist, the Catholic, or the Jewish church? How would you feel if a law were to be read to you which provided that unless you changed your religious belief and adopted some other, you would be burned to death out here on the hillside? You can hardly believe that such a thing would be possible in any age of the world; and yet never forget that the foregoing provision which I have read from the Constitution of the United States was the first declaration of the right of the people of a whole Nation to worship God according to their own will, their own conscience.

The declaration of this great right by the Constitution of the United States has been in full force ever since the adoption of the Constitution, not only as a National law, but similar provisions have been made the policy, usually by the Constitution, of every State in the Union. What a glorious thing it is to live in a Nation and in an age where no man, no state, and no power can tell you what to believe, or how to express your belief, what church you shall attend, or in what manner you shall express your religious faith.

Not only this, but this constitutional guaranty protects every one in his right to belong to no church if he so elects. The soul is free. No power can compel one to belong to any church, nor in any manner to hold or exercise religious faith, or religious duty or obligation. *In other words, men are free,* and this freedom, aside from any other guaranty of the Constitution, should make us all feel affection and veneration for this great charter of human liberty.

But freedom of worship is only one of the many rights and privileges guaranteed to the people—to all the people.

Another great natural right—God given right—is firmly and finally established:

"Congress shall make no law . . . . abridging the freedom of speech or of the press".[7]

Here again remember, when you are thinking of what you owe to your country, that this declaration of the Constitution was the first in all the history of the world by which a Nation guaranteed to all the people the right freely to express their thoughts in words or in writing. This was the first time the chains were taken from the human intellect. No one will ever be able to number the men and women who, throughout the history of the world, were condemned to death, because they dared to express their sentiments. If

Patrick Henry had delivered his famous speech in which he said, "Give me liberty, or give me death", in England rather than America, he would have been promptly punished. Hundreds of the colonists would have been hanged by the British government if they had expressed themselves in the mother country instead of in the new world. Kings to hold their power in the old world, to keep the people so terrorized that they would submit to their will, made the practice of hanging or beheading those who freely spoke their sentiments against the government.[8]

Of course under the old laws those who expressed their religious convictions in opposition to the state church by speech or writing were usually promptly imprisoned, hanged, or burned.

Now do not have any misunderstanding about this guaranty of freedom of speech and of the press. We often hear complaints of certain people about certain laws punishing those who abuse the privilege of free speech; but there is no law of State or Nation which prohibits the speaking or writing of anything in this country. Men may speak and write what they will; but there are some laws punishing those who abuse this great privilege to the injury of another person, or to the injury of the Nation. Of course no one would feel that it was right to allow another to write libelous articles about your neighbors. You would not feel that it would be right to permit some vile person to write false and vicious articles about your mother or your father; and yet any one may do so. They cannot be prohibited or enjoined from doing so, but they may be punished after doing so, after they have been tried in a court and found guilty of libel by a jury of their fellowmen.[9]

So if one writes a threatening letter to your father, telling him that he will kidnap his child unless he pays ten thousand dollars by a certain time, such person is exercising his constitutional right to freedom of expression, but no one would think that it was right to permit him thus to abuse his constitutional right without being punished for it; and consequently such person may be arrested and tried, and if found guilty, punished.

So in these later days it has been found wise, not to prohibit persons from giving expression to their views about our government, but to punish those who show by their words or writing that they are rebels against our government, endeavoring by their words to cause a revolution, to incite people to use force, bombs, or the torch to destroy our government.

No one can ever be punished for criticising our government, or any of the officers of our government, so long as he does not undertake to destroy our government, and I am sure that you would not think it right to permit any one to destroy the government controlled by ourselves which has brought to us so many blessings. Nearly every one agrees that if a person should use bombs or the torch in an effort to cause revolution and destroy our form of government, such a person should be punished; but there are a few who think that they should not be punished until they actually begin destruction. Of course we cannot agree with them. The man who goes out on the street corner and advocates the use of the bomb and the torch to destroy our government, who arouses passions willfully with the purpose of destroying the government, is doing just as much wrong as is done by the person who follows his advice and uses the bomb and the torch. In fact the man who advocates revolution and destruction, who preaches the use of the bomb and the torch, who plants the poison in the hearts of his fellowmen, and incites them to revolutionary action is more guilty of wrong than are those who, stirred by his appeals, carry out his wishes.

In punishing those who thus violate every principle of loyalty, patriotism, and right the constitutional provision is in no manner modified. The worst revolutionist has the freedom of speech and of the press guaranteed to him. The law which punishes him does so only because under the protection of the Constitution, he commits a crime against his country and against humanity.

America has done more than any other nation in the world in the cause of educating the common people. It should exercise care that the people should be educated in the true spirit of America, that their minds should not be poisoned by the vicious teachings of those, not Americans at heart, who seek to poison souls and rob the people of their patriotism and of their loyalty.

In the olden days so tyrannical was the king that in many instances when the people complained of their burdens and sought rights and privileges they were punished for daring to seek relief. The king would usually give them what he thought they ought to have and would not listen to complaints. One of the rights which the people always hoped for was the privilege of assembling, meeting together, talking over their troubles, drawing up a petition, signing, and presenting it, praying "a redress of grievance". When the representatives of the people met in the Constitutional Convention in Philadelphia they had before their minds the things that the people had suffered under old forms of government and it was their earnest effort to provide constitutional guaranties which would prevent the abuses to which the people were compelled to submit in the old world. Therefore one of the provisions of the Constitution of the United States is the following:

"Congress shall make no law . . . . abridging . . . . the right of the people peaceably to assemble, and to petition the Government for a redress of grievances."[10]

Under this constitutional guaranty the people have the right to assemble peaceably at any time or place, to talk over their troubles, and to draw up a petition to the government seeking relief from unjust burdens. Where they assemble peaceably there is no officer of the government and no court that can interfere with them; and when they petition the government they cannot be reprimanded or punished in any way. Of course under our representative government where the people themselves select those who make the laws, the necessity for assembling and drawing up petitions is not so great. Yet in Congress and in the legislatures of the various States nearly every day petitions come in from some body of people urging the adoption of a certain law or objecting to a certain proposed law. If you were in Congress or in the legislature you would probably see some member arise and say, "Mr. Speaker, I present the petition of the people of my district objecting to the passage of Bill No. 781, which I desire to have made part of the record", and the Speaker, who is the presiding officer, would respond in substance, "the request of the gentleman will be granted and the petition will be made part of the record".

What I desire especially to impress upon you this morning is the value of this right and the failure of our people to take advantage of the privilege granted. This being a government by the people and the laws being made by their agents, these agents of the people, members of Congress and of the State legislatures, cannot carry out the will of the people unless they know what the people want. Ask your father when you go home whether or not he has ever written to the member of Congress from this district telling him about some law he would like to have passed or about some proposed law he would like to see defeated. The truth is that there are large numbers of people in this city who do not even know the name of their congressman, or representative in the legislature of the State. They do not pay any attention to such things, yet when the legislature or Congress passes a law they are always ready to criticise and condemn, despite the fact that before it was passed they did not take interest enough to give an expression of their views to those who were trying to follow the wishes of the people. From time to time the people should assemble in every community to talk over government matters, their matters, the things that come most close to them in life. You will find men and women meeting every month in their lodges and clubs, discussing all sorts of things, music, art, and literature, but we find hardly any organized meetings for the discussion of the big things in life, our liberties, our rights, and our duties as citizens of this free republic. I hope to see the time when there will be community centers and regular assemblies, not for amusement but for serious discussion, serious thought, and earnest coöperation in the affairs of the city, State, and Nation. There is so much complaint in these days that it would be of great value at these assemblies to allow every person who has a grievance against the government or any branch of the government to present it for discussion. The rights and duties of each individual in government are of importance to every other person, and there should be frankness, honesty, and earnestness in every discussion of grievance and remedies, so that public sentiment may be developed. Government in a democracy is government by the sentiment of the people; and the sentiment of the people can only be created and manifested by talking over the things in which all people are interested—the problems of life, liberty, and happiness.

NOTES AND COMMENTS

1. Every right begets a duty. The more rights our government gives us, the more duties are imposed upon each one of us. In an absolute monarchy the people have very few rights and they also have very few duties to perform. In democracies like the United States the people have a right to participate in government, they also have the duty of becoming intelligent and becoming acquainted with the various details of the administration of government. When people have a right to participate in government, they have the duty of attending every election and casting an intelligent ballot. Where people have a right to make law, they must accept the duty of helping enforce law. Where people have freedom of religious belief and worship, they must refrain from interfering in the belief of other people. Where they have freedom of speech and press, they must protect other people in that same right. Where people have the right of trial in a legally constituted court of law, they must refrain from mob rule or from lynch law. The greater the privileges given a people by law, the greater are their duties to see that law is always respected and carefully enforced.

2. The government of the United States is a dual government. There is a State government within each State, which is supreme over the affairs of that State alone. Then there is a Federal government which is supreme and sovereign throughout the entire United States in all those affairs which the Federal Constitution gives to the control of the Federal government. The *police power* of a State is commonly defined as the power of a State to control all of its domestic internal affairs. The Federal government is not permitted to interfere with the police powers of the States.

3. "No state allows its government to dictate to any one what church he shall attend or compels him to contribute to the support of any church, the establishment of state churches being everywhere forbidden. No person is disqualified from holding office or exercising legal rights because of his religious views, although a very few states make belief in the Deity a requisite for holding certain state offices."—Hart's *Actual American Government*, Sec. 13.

4. Constitution of the United States, Amendment I.

5. Church and state are wholly separated in the United States. When a man takes office, no one asks him to what church he belongs, or what his faith is. If a man wants to believe in the religions of India or China, no officer of the National government has a right to interfere with him, providing he does not violate a law of the land. Religious tolerance is a growth. The Puritans who founded New England, although they fled to America because of religious persecutions, did not practice religious tolerance in the New World.

6. "The witchcraft craze at Salem, Massachusetts, in 1692, is commonly thought to have been the legitimate outgrowth of the gloomy religion of the Puritans. Nineteen persons were hanged or burned at the stake for having bewitched children. One was crushed to death under heavy weights because he would not confess that he was possessed of the devil. From the time of King John down to 1712, innocent lives were constantly sacrificed in England on this charge."—Thwaites's *The Colonies*, p. 190.

7. Constitution of the United States, Amendment I.

8. The first ten amendments to the Constitution of the United States are limitations on the powers of Congress, and these amendments do not in any way limit the powers of the several States. It is a fact, how-

ever, that practically all the States have incorporated these same amendments in their Constitutions thereby placing the same limitations upon their legislatures. A State may change its Constitution and thereby curtail freedom of speech and press as it may think necessary to protect its people, and some of the States have enacted laws forbidding anarchists to hold public meetings or to publish yellow journals in which they berate the government or instigate rebellion or sedition among the people. But the Federal government cannot pass any law abridging the freedom of speech or press except such as may be enacted under the war powers of the government when in actual war, such as was enacted in the Espionage Act of 1917.

9. Libel is defined as any statement printed, or written, or any picture or caricature that causes another person to be brought into hatred, contempt, or ridicule or to be shunned by his associates. Slander is any oral statement that causes another person to be brought into hatred, contempt, or ridicule, or to be shunned by his associates. In order to constitute either slander or libel the statement or utterance must be communicated to a third party.

"The right of citizens to petition the government to remove abuse was won in Europe only after many hard conflicts. It is not conceded in some European governments today, and men in those countries who lead in reforms and advocate democratic measures are often thrown into prison, banished, or exiled. This amendment to the Constitution was inserted to guard against the tyranny of officers, who might abuse the authority conferred upon them by the people."

10. Constitution of the United States, 1st Amendment.

"The right of assembly is coupled with the guaranty of the right to petition the government for a redress of grievances; but it is not to be understood as limited to that object. Without doubt assemblages for social, political or religious purposes are protected by such against legislative prohibition unless attended with circumstances rendering the exercise of the right inimical to public peace, security or welfare."— Emlin McClain, quoted in the *Cyclopedia of American Government*, Vol. I, p. 85.

"The right to assemble may be restricted so far as necessary to prevent its being exercised to promote unlawful purposes or in such manner as to result in public inconvenience."—*Cyclopedia of American Government*, Vol. I, p. 85.

"The provision to the amendment to the Federal Constitution is a limitation only on the powers of the Federal Government and does not apply to the several states. The states have largely copied the same provision into their constitutions."

"The right of petition is important as recognizing a lawful occasion for the assembly of the people and in connection with the guaranty of freedom of speech and the press. The subject matter of a petition cannot be made the basis for a prosecution for public or private libel if it is kept within the limits of the privilege accorded."—*Cyclopedia of American Government*, Vol. II, p. 675.

"Through the right of petition the people have a means of informing their law-makers of their wishes and of guiding public opinion."

"The rules of the national House of Representatives provide that members having petitions to present may deliver them to the clerk and the petition, except such as, in the judgment of the speaker, are of an obscene or insulting character, shall be entered upon the journal."—Emlin McClain, quoted in the *Cyclopedia of American Government*, Vol. II, p. 675.

ELEMENTARY QUESTIONS

1. Which colonists came to America to avoid religious persecution?
2. Why do people fight and die for their religious beliefs?
3. In what ways were people persecuted for their religious beliefs?
4. Where was the first statute granting absolute freedom of worship passed?
5. Why is it a good thing to have freedom of speech?
6. Name some famous Americans who have been outspoken in saying what they thought.
7. Can you publish in the paper a statement that Mr. X is a burglar? If so, can you be punished if your statement is not true? If so, how can you have freedom of speech?
8. Is the Constitution of the United States in force in all the States of the Union?
9. Are there other constitutions which the people of different States must observe?
10. Why did the people want the right to assemble?
11. Do you know of any countries where they do not allow it?
12. Do you know of anyone who ever sent a petition to a State legislature? To Congress? What was it like?
13. How many assemblies of people and petitions help to make our representatives do what we want them to do?

ADVANCED QUESTIONS

A. Name the places in the world, where to-day there is religious persecution.
B. Describe the conditions in Armenia.
C. What are the real advantages of religious liberty?
D. Just how would it affect a person if freedom of speech were not allowed?
E. How may the right to freedom of speech be abused?
F. During the recent war, men were punished for what they said under what is known as the Espionage Act. How can this be reconciled with freedom of speech?
G. Discuss the method of organizing a community meeting.
H. Discuss the method of preparing a petition.
I. Suppose the opinion of the meeting should be divided, what should be the procedure?
J. Plan a method to make the people talk more about government.
K. What are the dangers of a lack of interest in the affairs of government?
L. How will a congressman represent the wishes of the people if he receives no petitions?
M. Write a paper on the following:
    The Story of the Pilgrims
    Roger Williams and the Providence Colony
    Lord Baltimore
    Thomas Jefferson and Religious Liberty
    Censorship of the Press and Freedom of Speech
    What to do with an Anarchist Meeting
    Socialist Papers
    The Importance of the Right of Petition
    Keeping in Touch with our Representatives
    Some Petitions I have Seen.
    Things for Which We Should Petition the Legislature

X

MILITARY PROVISIONS

RIGHTS OF CITIZENS TO BEAR ARMS—RESTRICTIONS ON
QUARTERING SOLDIERS IN HOMES

Again we find the framers of the Constitution looking back
into the past at abuses imposed upon the people by kingly
power. They inserted in the Constitution the following provision:

*"A well regulated Militia, being necessary to the security
of a free State, the right of the people to keep and bear Arms,
shall not be infringed."*[1]

They were making a government of free States. They did
not wish to see the National government become the master
of the States nor the master of the people. They believed
that the government should be the servant and not the master. They wanted to have the power in the hands of the people of the States to protect their rights if they ever should
be invaded by force; and therefore they furnished to the people of all the States the guaranty that the States should have
the right to have militia, that is, soldiers organized to maintain order and to defend the State, if necessary, against abuse
of power; and they guaranteed to the people the right to
bear arms lawfully.

If you read the history of the old world you will find many
instances of soldiers entering the homes of the people to
search for fire arms or other weapons, taking them away,
possibly punishing those who had them. The people are
guarded by our Constitution against any such conduct on the
part of soldiers or representatives of the National government.
Of course this right, like the right of free speech, may be
abused and when abused punishment may be imposed. For

instance, it is dangerous to the good order of a community that persons should carry concealed weapons and therefore in every State there is some law concerning this. If a man should walk down the street here with a loaded revolver in his pocket he could be arrested and imprisoned, or fined, but in this State a man could walk down the street with a shot gun in his hands or any other weapon where it is exposed so people could see it. A law against carrying concealed weapons imposes no burden upon any law-abiding citizen. There are regulations, of course, permitting certain persons to carry weapons concealed, police officers, a sheriff, and other peace officers; and there is a law under which any person of good moral character may make application for authority to carry concealed weapons which will be granted under certain restrictions. Some States require a bond to be filed guaranteeing good conduct. Persons who have to carry large sums of money, express messengers upon the trains, post office employees who carry registered mail, and other persons may be granted the privilege of carrying concealed weapons. The laws regarding carrying concealed weapons differ from State to State, the punishment in some being a term in the penitentiary.

But in all this we find only regulation and careful provision to help maintain order and peace; and with it all we find the absolute right given by the Constitution to the people to maintain their State militia and to keep and bear arms within reasonable regulations which may be provided by the different States.

Then we find a strict guaranty of the Constitution against an abuse which was common in the old world. You know before America came into being the strength of a government was the power of a government. The people were ruled by force; they were kept in constant fear. When this Nation was organized it was the hope of the founders that we could have laws so just that people would have love for their country and respect for its laws, so that we would not have to inspire fear in the hearts of the people in order to make them obey. Laws should be obeyed not because of fear, but because of respect, because of a sense of duty. Laws should be obeyed because we know that laws are necessary to protect our own liberties. We know that without law, liberty is impossible.

So that when the Constitution was framed, reflecting upon the abuses of the old world, the makers of the Constitution inserted this guaranty:

"No Soldier shall, in time of peace, be quartered in any house, without the consent of the Owner, nor in time of war, but in a manner to be prescribed by law."[2]

In the olden days the military power was supreme. The soldier was part of the military power. The ordinary citizen was compelled to submit to many of the wishes of the soldiers in times of peace as well as in times of war. In reading the history of the world you will find that soldiers exercised the right to enter the homes of the people and demand food and shelter. Of course the people, being in fear of the military power, would not think of refusing anything demanded; but the people of America, under our Constitution, are supreme. The soldier is subject to the people, not the people subject to the soldier. While we must respect those who are the defenders of our country, we must also respect our own rights and privileges. And every soldier, general or private, must also respect our rights and privileges. No soldier can enter any home, no matter how humble, without the consent of the owner, except in times of war. Even in times of war he cannot enter except under circumstances and conditions prescribed by law. The law being made by the people, they will be protected against abuse. Of course in times of war every one should be glad to give freely of what he has for the soldiers of his country, but in times of peace in this country the soldier, under our Constitution, understands that the home is sacred and that he has no right there unless the owner invites him to enter.

I wonder if the people realize what these guaranties mean to them. I wonder if they understand how earnestly and how carefully those who framed the Constitution endeavored to protect the sacred rights of every man, woman, and child in this country.

NOTES AND COMMENTS

1. Constitution of the United States, Amendment II.

"This right to keep and bear arms, although stated in connection with the militia, is held broad enough to cover the keeping and carrying of such weapons as are suitable for self-defense, or defense of the home. But the keeping of unusual weapons, or the carrying of unusual weapons in an unusual manner, as by having them concealed on the person, may be prohibited."—Bouvier's *Law Dictionary*, Vol. I, p. 165.

"This amendment, like the other eight amendments to the Federal Constitution, does not apply to the States, and a State may legislate as it pleases regarding the carrying and using of arms. Many states prevent the carrying of arms of any kind except with legal permission given through the proper officer for stated specific reasons."

"The amendment means no more than that this right shall not be infringed by Congress. Police protection of the people is left to the States."

2. One of the grievances of the colonists stated in the Declaration of Independence was the quartering of large bodies of armed troops in the colonies, but the guaranty found in the Federal Constitution and in many State Constitutions is that soldiers shall not in times of peace be quartered upon private persons. This guaranty has respect to the recognition of the right of every man not to be unwarrantably disturbed or intruded upon in his home. "Every man's house is his castle."

ELEMENTARY QUESTIONS

1. Why did the Germans refuse to allow the Belgians to keep and bear arms?
2. Why is this right important to us?
3. Ask some soldier who fought in France to tell you about how soldiers quartered in the village. Would you like to see this in America? Why not?
4. What rights has a soldier in time of peace to demand admitttauce to a house, or to demand food?
5. In time of war under what conditions may a soldier be quartered in any house?
6. Where is the whole power of government in America? Where is it in a kingdom or monarchy?
7. Do you know the name of your congressman?
8. When should a person be allowed to carry weapons?

ADVANCED QUESTIONS

A. What is the importance of the right of keeping and bearing arms?

B. What is the status of the National Guard in your locality? What are its duties? What is its purpose?

C. What is the fundamental objection to the quartering of soldiers on a population in time of peace?

D. Write a paper on the following:
   The Right to Bear Arms
   The Evils of Quartering of Soldiers
   The Purpose of the National Guard
   How the Soldiers Were Quartered in France

XI

SEARCH WARRANT AND INDICTMENT

THE HOME PROTECTED AGAINST UNLAWFUL SEARCH AND SEIZURE—GRAND JURY INDICTMENT REQUIRED

Following the provision that we last discussed that no soldier shall in time of peace be quartered in any house without the consent of the owner, nor in time of war except in a manner prescribed by law, we find the Constitution making a most positive provision guarding the sacredness of the home, the sacredness of the person, and the things belonging to each person. In the olden days the people had to submit to the most brutal conduct. A man might think some one had stolen his ring or his watch. Suspecting a neighbor, and being the stronger, or assembling his friends, or some officers, he might enter the neighbor's home, search all through the house among papers, in the desks, and in every trunk and other place where personal belongings were kept, might search the person himself, his pockets, and clothing.

Of course you can easily understand that the people who were thus abused would resent such actions. In England the people in early days had protested and had secured some guaranties from the king against these outrages, but the first absolute written guaranty of the full rights of the people was when the following provision was inserted in our Constitution:

"The right of the people to be secure in their persons, houses, papers, and effects, against unreasonable searches and seizures, shall not be violated, and no Warrants shall issue, but upon probable cause, supported by Oath or affirmation, and particularly describing the place to be searched, and the persons or things to be seized."[1]

Of course it is apparent that so long as we have crimes committed the wrongdoer must be punished. Wrongdoers naturally try to conceal the evidence of their crimes: the murderer seeks to hide the revolver, the thief seeks to hide the money, the bonds, or the jewels. So it is necessary, in order to find criminals and to recover valuable things they may have taken, to have the privilege of searching persons or houses. But the thing which the Constitution guarantees is that no such search shall be made except upon warrants issued by some court, which are commands to a peace officer to seize a certain person (arrest him) or to search a certain house or other place for things which might aid in administering justice. No warrants shall be issued by any court until some one has appeared and filed a solemn statement under oath showing some reasonable grounds for believing that the search or seizure will disclose evidence of the offense. The place must be described. The things or the persons to be seized must be described. A warrant issued by any court, no matter how high, without such a sworn statement being presented, is void and in violation of the rights of every person under the Constitution. The courts are often called upon to enforce this right of the people. The home, especially under our Constitution, is recognized as sacred. "Every man's house is his castle" and wherever, without the proper warrant, search or seizure is made, the court will promptly punish the wrongdoer and if something has been seized or taken possession of wrongfully the court will order it returned. Even though valuable as evidence of guilt, the court will not permit it to be used, if it has been seized in violation of the guaranty of the Constitution.

No matter how humble the home, whether it be owned or rented, whether it have one room or a dozen, it stands exactly the same under this constitutional provision, and is guarded against "unreasonable searches and seizures". No matter how poor the owner, he can stand at his door and defy all the officers of State or government, yes, and all the soldiers of the republic, defy them to enter until the provisions of the Constitution of the United States shall have been complied with.

Now, we come to guaranties of the right of the people to protection against any trial, except the same be conducted in accordance with the guaranties of the Constitution. These guaranties are for all persons, young or old, rich or poor. You know sometimes the innocent are charged with grave crimes. A crime is committed in the darkness of the night. The criminal has fled. The first duty of the officers of the government—the servants of the people—is to find the criminal so that he may be punished for his wrongdoing. This is not an easy task, and no matter how careful officers may be, mistakes are sometimes made and innocent persons are arrested and charged with the offense. Bring this home to yourself, because every one of these constitutional guaranties are for you, for each of you, for your father, mother, brothers, and sisters. Keep this in mind. Do not consider them as applying to somebody away off, some stranger in whom you have no interest. *They apply to you.*

Now suppose that to-night a murder should be committed, and to-morrow your father should be arrested and charged with the crime of which he was entirely innocent. It will be very important to him that he should have a fair chance, a fair trial. His liberty would be at stake, and liberty under the Constitution is a sacred thing. Thinking of liberty his mind would naturally turn to the Constitution, and if he examined it, he would find the following guaranty:

"No person shall be held to answer for a capital, or otherwise infamous crime, unless on a presentment or indictment of a Grand Jury, except in cases arising in the land or naval

forces, or in the Militia, when in actual service in time of War or public danger."[2]

Now you do not understand this, do you? And yet it is very simple. When a man is arrested, he is brought before the court for trial. But how, and before whom shall he be tried?

Remember that in America the enforcement of law is in the hands of the people. Remember that this is a government by the people and that the chief purpose of government is to protect the liberties of the people. Here is your father's liberty at stake. If he should be convicted of having committed this murder, he might be hanged or sent to prison for life, so it is very important to him that the investigation into the charge against him shall be conducted in the right manner.

Under this constitutional guaranty which is also included in your State Constitution, there is no court and no judge in the United States big enough or powerful enough to call your father before the court for trial until he has been indicted by a grand jury. A grand jury, generally composed of twelve or more men selected from ordinary citizens, is brought together every term of court. They sit in a room by themselves and hear evidence as to the commission of offenses. They have no power to find a man guilty or not guilty. Their power and their duty is to decide whether the evidence brought before them is sufficient to justify putting the accused man on trial for the offense. They hear the witnesses for the State or government. The defendant is not brought before them personally, nor is he represented in any way. It is simply a secret investigation. If these men upon this investigation decide the evidence is not sufficient to warrant the trial of a man, he is discharged. He cannot be put on trial before the court. Before the court can proceed the grand jury must first say that the man shall be tried. The people thus have in their hands the power of protecting the innocent, and the power of instituting proceedings against the guilty. The grand jury brings in its report by an "indictment" which is merely a written statement to the court that the grand jury believes the defendant should be put upon trial for a certain offense. When this indictment is brought in, the defendant is called before the court, the charge is read to him, and he is then required to say whether he is guilty or not guilty. If he says that he is not guilty, then preparation must be made for a trial in the court, before a petit jury, a trial jury, which we will consider later. The thing I want to impress upon you now is the care with which the framers of the Constitution guarded the right of your father to have an investigation by a body of citizens before he can be brought up for trial for this murder which has been committed. He cannot be dragged by officers before some court and forced to go hurriedly through a form of trial only to be found guilty. The proceedings must be deliberate and careful. The Constitution guards him against danger of conviction without substantial proof of his guilt.

There are a few minor offenses, sometimes called misdemeanors, and there are violations of city ordinances, in which an indictment is not necessary, but an indictment by a grand jury is necessary whenever the crime is infamous or capital; that is, generally speaking, when punishment would involve imprisonment in the penitentiary or the taking of life by hanging or otherwise. You will understand this better as we consider the trial before the petit jury.

You may think it is difficult to learn all about grand juries, the number of jurors, and the manner in which they are sworn to perform their duties. I do not blame you. But bear in mind I am not insisting that you shall learn all these details. Of course the more knowledge we have about these matters the better. But *the important thing* is that you shall

learn that away back more than one hundred and thirty
years ago the people of America in framing the Constitution of our country, by written guaranties, made this a government by the people. Knowing that the most sacred thing
on this earth is human liberty, they sought to guard it by
providing every possible safeguard which would protect the
innocent from unjust conviction. They trusted the people.
While courts were provided, the power to accuse the humblest
human being living under the American flag of a grave offense and bring him before a court for trial was reserved to
the people themselves.

Grand juries are merely representatives or agents of the
people. As they sit in court they are exercising some of the
highest and most important duties exercised by men. Grand
jurors and petit jurors hold in their hands the liberty of their
fellowmen.

It is these great truths I wish to impress upon you. I want
you to have the knowledge, but more than this, I want you
to have the spirit, the spirit of confidence in your government, and the spirit of gratitude that you live in America
where the people rule, where the people not only make the
law, but enforce it.

NOTES AND COMMENTS

1. Constitution of the United States, Amendment IV.

"One of the most serious grievances of the colonists was, the assertion
and exercise of a prerogative of the crown to issue warrants for searching private premises in order to obtain evidence of political offenses. This
had been the subject of controversy in England and was made the basis
of a protest in Massachusetts by James Otis against the Writs of Assistance which were in effect, general warrants."—*Cyclopedia of American
Government*, Vol. III, p. 654.

"The privilege contended for was that the privacy of the dwelling
house should not be invaded by public officers without the consent of
the owner save for the purpose of making an arrest, and then only by
an officer of the law—who carried a warrant giving him such authority."
—Emlin McClain, quoted in the *Cyclopedia of American Government*,
Vol. III, p. 654.

The protection afforded by the constitutional provision is against attempts made under the disguise of public process to pry into private

affairs on mere suspicion that a crime has been committed or contemplated.

The principle of this guaranty is being violated if the postal authorities open sealed letters in the mail to discover whether improper use of the mail is being made. It is also violated by compelling the production of private papers of the defendant in a criminal prosecution.

A warrant is not always necessary to arrest an individual. For example, a police officer does not need a warrant in order to arrest a person who is violating a law in his presence, or a person whom he has good reason to think has committed a felony.—*Cyclopedia of American Government*, Vol. III, p. 655.

2. Constitution of the United States, Amendment V.

"A *capital crime* is such crime as the law declares punishable by death penalty."—Bouvier's *Law Dictionary*, Vol. I, p. 284.

"An *infamous crime* is such crime as the law declares punishable by imprisonment in a state prison."

A grand jury, or an indictment, or a presentment jury, or an inquest jury, is a jury (differing as to numbers in different States) for the purpose of investigating alleged crimes. If, upon investigation, the jury believes the accused person has either committed the act or has had a part in the crime, it will draw up a formal accusation in writing. This accusation is called an indictment and is presented to the court. In a few States a person may be brought to trial for violation of a law of the State upon information filed by the prosecuting attorney.

A *petit jury*, or *trial jury*, is a jury of twelve men selected by the court—according to a law determining the manner—to hear the accusation against the person charged along with the evidence submitted during the trial in court. After hearing the evidence and receiving from the judge instructions concerning the law governing the case, the jury will determine whether the accused person is guilty or not. The Federal government, and most of the States, require a unanimous verdict. If the jury disagrees they report such to the court (the judge) and they are dismissed and the case may be tried again with a different jury.

"Constitutional guaranties of the right of trial for crime only on indictment by a grand jury, imply a common law grand jury of whose number at least twelve men concur in finding the indictment, but by provision in state constitutions a smaller number of grand jurors than required by common law and concurrence of a smaller number than twelve in the finding of an indictment may be authorized."

"A grand jury affords a safeguard against the unwarranted ignominy of being put on public trial for an offense which there is no reasonable ground to believe the accused has committed."

"The grand jury is to investigate the cases of those who have been arrested and held under preliminary information on oath by private accusers; and it may also investigate cases of supposed crime of which it has knowledge or to which its attention may be called by the public prosecuting officer. Its proceedings are secret and its members are sworn not to subsequently divulge them."—McClain's *Constitutional Law*.

ELEMENTARY QUESTIONS

1. In the olden days how could a strong man abuse one suspected of stealing?
2. What would he be compelled to do to-day?
3. Why are the guaranties regarding trials important to you?

4. Who may accuse or charge a person with a crime?
5. Is a person charged with a crime necessarily guilty?
6. What is a grand jury? What is its purpose?
7. How are members of a grand jury servants of the people?
8. Is a search warrant valid if no sworn statement has been filed?
9. What are the rights of the owner, if a search is made without proper warrant or papers?
10. State the guaranty of the Constitution with reference to indictment by a grand jury.
11. Is the session of a grand jury secret or public?
12. Is the defendant present before the grand jury during the investigation?
13. What is meant by "indictment"?
14. What is done when the grand jury returns an indictment?
15. What offenses may be prosecuted without an indictment?

ADVANCED QUESTIONS

A. Discuss the procedure of securing a search warrant?
B. If we had no guaranty of security of property rights what effect would this have with reference to working, earning, and saving?
C. How is the fact that we have a grand jury an evidence of the care with which our government guards our rights?
D. What is a heinous crime?
E. Write a paper on:
Early Abuses of Power in Search and Seizure
Some Interesting Violations of this Right
The Grand Jury as an Evidence That the People Rule
An Account of the Work of One Grand Jury

XII

RIGHTS OF ACCUSED

ACQUITTAL BY JURY FINAL—ACCUSED NOT COMPELLED TO BE A WITNESS

Now keeping in mind that this is a personal matter with each one of us, that we are talking about our own rights, that some day our liberties may be in danger, let us take up the next guaranty of the Constitution: *"nor shall any person be subject for the same offence to be twice put in jeopardy of life or limb".*[1]

I am sure you do not know what that means. I am sure there is not one of you who ever dreamed that such a thing might happen to you as to be "twice put in jeopardy of life or limb". This is very important and likewise very simple. In the olden days, in the old world, many a man was tried for a crime in court and found not guilty, and then later was arrested and put on trial again and found guilty. Suppose your father, as I said the other day, should be arrested, although he were innocent. Suppose he were indicted by this grand jury and brought on for trial. He would be compelled to hire a lawyer, if he were able to, and get ready for trial. The trial would come on, and days or possibly weeks might be spent in examining witnesses. Finally the case would close and the jury would bring in a verdict of "not guilty". It would be an expensive proceeding. Perhaps it would take all the money he had saved. It would not only be expensive but it would be a hard strain upon him, your mother, the other children, and yourself. It is a very serious matter for an innocent man to be tried for murder. Still the verdict of "not guilty" comes in and you are all full of joy to realize that his life and liberty have been saved. Now suppose it were possible that within a couple of weeks afterwards he could again be arrested, indicted, put on trial. All of the family would again be subjected to worry and sorrow. You do not think it would be just, do you? It would not be right. Of course it wouldn't be right, but men in the olden days have been compelled to submit to such injustices. So when the Constitution was adopted this guaranty which I just read was put in there, so that for any offense against the United States no man can be tried again after acquittal. Once a jury of his fellowmen, his neighbors, brings in a verdict of "not guilty" that ends forever any prosecution for the same offense. He is free and there is no power in the United States nor any of its officers to call him again for trial for that offense. Most of the States have a like constitutional guaranty.

Then there is another important guaranty: *"nor shall (he) be compelled in any criminal case to be a witness against himself"*.[2]

I wonder if you have ever heard of the days when men were tortured to make them confess. I wonder if you ever heard of the rack where men were stretched, almost torn limb from limb, or of the days when men were hung up by their thumbs, in order to compel them to admit their guilt of some crime. Have you read of the burning of the soles of men's feet? Or the application of red hot irons to other parts of the body in order to extort a confession? Well those were common things in some of the countries in the days before America was born. Men would be arrested, charged with an offense, and then an effort would be made to torture them into confessing to the crime. And often where no such brutal torture was employed, men were brought into court, put on the stand, threatened, examined, and cross examined by lawyers to try to gain admissions which might help to prove their guilt. Of course this was all wrong. It was brutal. It was a violation of human right. When the

Constitution of the United States was framed this great abuse of human privilege was absolutely barred by the provision, that no one can "be compelled in any criminal case to be a witness against himself". In this country, when a man is brought into court charged with a crime, it is the duty of the government to prove his guilt. This proof must be by the sworn testimony of witnesses of certain facts or circumstances, aside from any statement or admission by the defendant. He cannot be compelled to be a witness at all. If he so wishes, however, he may be a witness for himself. This privilege was denied him under the English practice for generations, and even in this country in many of the States until a comparatively recent time; but never since the Constitution was adopted could any person charged with a crime against the United States be compelled to testify to any fact or circumstance in relation to the crime. Not only can he sit in the court room and listen to the stories told against him, but he is guaranteed this right by protection against any threats or inducements outside of court and before the trial which would lead him to say anything against his innocence. Every judge in criminal courts has been compelled at times to refuse to admit in evidence before the jury certain statements or alleged confessions. You may see in the paper where some man has been arrested for breaking into a bank or committing some other offense, and it may be further stated that the defendant has confessed that he broke into the bank. Naturally you then say to yourself that he will be found guilty. Well this constitutional guaranty not only protects him in court but protects him out of court. He cannot be compelled to give answers after his arrest while he is in jail, or even if he is at liberty under bond, which can be used against him upon the trial. Of course a person charged with a crime may waive this constitutional guaranty. He may voluntarily say that he wants to tell his story, and if he does so without any inducement, promises, or threats it may be admitted against him when the trial comes. Otherwise not. To be admitted, it must appear to be absolutely voluntary and of his own free will. If it appears that the confession has been induced by promises of lighter sentence or "that it will be easier for him", or if any other inducement is used to get him to consent to make his statement, such statement cannot be used in evidence because of his constitutional guaranty. Many times I have seen the court refuse to admit proof of an alleged confession of a defendant, and I could see that the jury trying the case and the people sitting in the court room were surprised that the judge would not admit such proof even when the confession was signed by the defendant; but the jury and the people did not happen to think of this constitutional provision. Perhaps they had never heard of it. Every judge is sworn to uphold and defend the Constitution. No judge can permit any provision of the Constitution to be violated if he can help it. A man is on trial before him. A written confession is offered in evidence to help convict him. The defendant's attorneys claim that the confession was not voluntary but was induced by threats or promises. The court then makes inquiry and hears the witnesses upon this question, and if the court finds that the confession was not the voluntary act of the defendant, the same will be excluded because the Constitution provides that no man "shall be compelled in any criminal case to be a witness against himself".

Let us turn again to the false accusation against your father. He is charged with murder. He is on trial before a jury. The attorney for the government pulls a paper out of his pocket and offers it in evidence. It appears to be signed by your father. Your father's attorney objects to having it considered by the jury for the reason that the policemen took your father into a cell in the jail, and threatened that they would beat him with their clubs unless he would sign a paper telling how he committed the offense, and that in terror he signed the paper. At this point, the court would hear the statements of your father, and other evidence, and if it appeared that there were any threats of any kind used to get your father to sign the paper, it would not be admitted in evidence at all. Your father would only claim his constitutional rights as an American, and they would not be denied to him.

There are notable instances in which confessions were made and signed by innocent parties, who were discouraged because the facts seemed to be all against them, who felt that they were certain to be convicted, and that their punishment would be lighter if they would make a confession. Under this impression they made and signed a confession. It was afterward found that the confession was false and that they were innocent of the crime. This constitutional guaranty protects against any injustice of this kind.

These careful efforts of the makers of the Constitution to guard the liberties of the most humble persons must impress us with the earnestness of their efforts to make this a free country, where no one shall be deprived of his life or liberty except where proven guilty, after a most carefully guarded trial.

Isn't it fine to live in a country where the people have a Constitution written in such simple language that even the little children can read it? I want every one, even the smallest child, to understand that every line of the Constitution was written to guard and protect each one of us, young and old, against injustice and wrong. These safeguards cannot be taken away except by the people themselves. The President cannot change the Constitution. Congress cannot change it. Judges cannot change it. No one but the men and women of America can alter it in the least.

NOTES AND COMMENTS

1. Constitution of the United States, Amendment V.

"The rule of procedure generally recognized is that when an accused person has been put on trial under a valid indictment in a court having jurisdiction of the case, and a jury has been empaneled and sworn to try the case and give a verdict, and a verdict of *not guilty* is given—the accused cannot be again put on trial for the same crime, or any included crime for which he might have been convicted in that prosecution."—*Cyclopedia of American Government*, Vol. II, p. 251.

"A verdict of not guilty is conclusive and the defendant must be discharged. If however he is convicted, he may in some instances appeal the case to a higher court for review and that is not being again put in jeopardy."—Emlin McClain, quoted in the *Cyclopedia of American Government*, Vol. II, p. 251.

"Jeopardy is complete when the court proceeds with a jury to ascertain the defendant's guilt."

"As the criminal jurisdiction of the Federal Court extends only to offenses against the Federal laws, and no prosecution for such offenses can be entertained in the state courts—it follows that there can be no questions of former jeopardy as between a federal and a state court."—*Cyclopedia of American Government*, Vol. II, p. 251.

2. Constitution of the United States, Amendment V.

In our own early colonies persons were frequently tortured to compel them to give evidence against themselves or against other people, but at that time the colonies were still under British authority.

An instance was recently reported of a man appearing before a sheriff and confessing to the commission of five different murders in as many different places in a western State. Upon investigation it was found that murders had been committed in these places about the time he confessed to having committed the crimes, so he was arrested and held by the sheriff. Upon further investigation it was discovered that he was mentally unbalanced and having read of all these crimes he imagined he had committed them. He was released from arrest and was committed to a hospital for the insane. In this instance an innocent man might have been executed if his own testimony had been sufficient to convict him.

If a person confesses to having committed a crime and the facts as stated are found to be correct, he may then be convicted of the crime, but the conviction is made on the basis of the evidence disclosed by his confession and not on the confession itself. Having made a confession the officers may then from the facts told by the accused find other facts sufficient to convict without offering the confession in evidence.

"A confession is not admissible in evidence where it is obtained by temporal inducement, by threats, promise or hope of favor held out to the party in respect of his escape from the charge against him, by a person in authority."—Bouvier's *Law Dictionary*, Vol. I, p. 387.

"When an inducement destroys a confession it must be held out by a person in authority."

ELEMENTARY QUESTIONS

1. Show how being put on trial again and again for the same offense would be an injustice.
2. Why is it right to have the verdict of "not guilty" final?

3. What would be the result if it were not final?
4. Why is this of *particular* advantage to the poor man?
5. Why should no man be compelled to be a witness against himself?
6. Why do they allow a man to be a witness if he so desires?
7. What is the importance of the guaranty protecting the defendant from being examined as a witness?
8. When a person is indicted for an offense, what is the duty of the government with reference to proof of guilt?
9. How is guilt proven in court?
10. When may a confession made outside of court be introduced as evidence?
11. Why would anyone accused of a crime confess guilt, when in fact he might not be guilty at all?
12. Can the President or Congress or a judge change any of the provisions of the Constitution?

ADVANCED QUESTIONS

A. Discuss the democracy of the provision that the verdict of "not guilty" is final while that of "guilty" may not of necessity be final?
B. Why are confessions wrung from frightened or tortured men likely to be untrustworthy?
C. Why should the "Third Degree" methods be prohibited?
D. Write a paper on the following:
The Third Degree
Early Cases of Torturing Accused Persons
The Burdens, Disadvantages, and Injustice of Permitting a Retrial After A Verdict of "Not Guilty"
Methods Sometimes Used to Secure a Confession of Guilt

XIII

LIFE, LIBERTY, AND PROPERTY

RIGHTS PROTECTED BY DUE PROCESS OF LAW—PROPERTY TAKEN FOR PUBLIC USE

The three great things which every man, woman, and child cherishes are life, liberty, and property. We see in every one of these guaranties how careful the people who made the Constitution were to see that these valuable things were sacredly guarded.

It is stated in the Constitution that:

"No person shall . . . . be deprived of life, liberty, or property, without due process of law".[1]

You can understand how important this is if you will realize how in the olden days people were so brutally treated by their fellowmen, especially by those in power who happened to represent the government. Have you ever read the story of the Bastile, a prison in which hundreds of French people were thrown without a trial, in which many were murdered and many kept in dark cells chained to the floor for years? Have you ever read the story of the Tower in London, where men were imprisoned and murdered without a trial by any court and without an investigation by any one, often without the knowledge of their closest friends? Have you ever read about how the property of people was taken away from them without trial or investigation to be turned over to the king or to some of his friends? Until you have read something of the past, and realize how people suffered, how they lost their lives, their liberty, and their property, you will never realize the wisdom of those who framed our Constitution, nor the affection which they had for the people of America in protecting them against such horrible treatment.

No person's property can be taken, no person's life can be taken, no person's liberty can be taken under our Constitution without due process of law. We do not need to discuss the meaning of "due process of law". You will learn more about this later, as you study more fully the details of the Constitution. It is sufficient now to say that no person's life, liberty, or property can be taken away from him without his consent, except by a trial before a legal court, in which the person shall have the right to a fair hearing. He must have notice of the charge or claim made against him. He must have a chance to appear in person. He must have the right to employ attorneys to represent him. He must have the privilege of bringing in witnesses to tell the truth about the charges that may be made. There must be a decision by the court after a speedy public trial. In all the States of this country any one is entitled to such a trial, and he is also, in case of defeat, entitled to appeal and present his case to a different and a higher court. These courts are the courts of the people, selected by the people, and neither government nor individuals have any right to take away anyone's life, liberty, or property unless the people by and through their courts shall so find and do.

Then we find the following constitutional provision: *"nor shall private property be taken for public use, without just compensation."*

Of course the government at times must have property which may belong to a private person. The public must at times take property belonging to an individual. Property may be taken, even when the owner will not consent to it, when it is taken for public use. One man's property cannot be taken by the government and given to another person. Government buildings must be erected and land must be obtained for such purposes. The public must have railroads, and a railroad can only be built when land is obtained for what is called the right of way. Sometimes a railroad must run through lots or farms belonging to private owners. The higher right of the public to these conveniences, these necessities, requires that when necessary the private individual must give up his right of ownership to these higher public uses. But even for the Nation, or the State, or railway, or for any other public use, not one foot of land may be taken from the poorest man in the country unless he is first fully paid its value therefor. Usually, of course, the owner will sell his property for such purpose at a fair price, but, if he is stubborn and will not do so, or if a fair price cannot be agreed upon then the government of the State or of the Nation, or the agents of the State or of the Nation may take such property by first having its value fixed by a commission, or a jury, composed of the neighbors of the owner. Where the amount fixed by such commission or jury is not satisfactory to the owner of the property, he may appeal to the court and have a trial, usually a jury trial, in which he can bring his witnesses and prove the value of his property, so that he will finally receive its full, fair, just value.

By this constitutional guaranty every person is well guarded in his ownership and possession of property. In countries existing before America not much attention was paid to the rights of property owners. If the king or emperor should demand possession of a certain piece of property the owner had little to say about it. He received his orders and obeyed them, because he was afraid of the power of the government. The government could pay or not as it pleased. But this period of wrong and injustice was ended, so far as the people of America were concerned, when the Constitution became the final power in this land.

There are a few people in this country who seek to have private ownership of property abolished. No law taking away the right to own property can ever come into force in this country until the people by their votes change the Constitution. The Constitution stands guard over the farms, the homes, the money, and all forms of personal property. It guards the cottage of the widow with the same jealous care that it does the ten-story building of the bank. No person and no power can interfere with the right to accumulate property and to hold it, provided only it is honestly obtained.

NOTES AND COMMENTS

1. Constitution of the United States, Amendment V.

This is a part of the fifth amendment to the Federal Constitution, and the fourteenth is an expansion of it, and assumes that the man charged with the crime is innocent until proven guilty. The old standard set in Europe was that a person charged with crime was considered guilty until he was proven innocent. All citizens, whether native or foreign born, have the protection of this amendment.—Bouvier's *Law Dictionary*, Vol. I, p. 622.

Previous to 1679 in England an accused person could be detained in prison for months or even for years and had no recourse to the courts, but might be thus detained in prison upon a mere charge brought by some one jealous of him and without real reason. In that year the people demanded that Parliament should give relief against unjust or false imprisonment, and Parliament enacted the Habeas Corpus Act. The provisions of this notable act require that a person imprisoned may demand a preliminary hearing and learn the cause of his being seized and imprisoned. Either he or his friends or relatives could go before a judge of a court and demand a *writ of habeas corpus*. Such writ was issued by a judge and directed to the jailer or the person detaining the accused and he was compelled to bring the accused person before the court and show legal reason why that person should be detained. If no such cause or reason could be given, the accused person must be set at liberty. The guaranty of the right to a writ of habeas corpus under our Constitution is considered hereafter. See page 144.

Due process of law may be defined as "according to the law of the place in which the trial is held". It means in this instance that no person may be deprived of life, liberty, or property without the right of judicial trial. *Due process of law* does not necessarily mean *jury trial*. If a jury trial is the legally recognized method of trying such case, then jury trial is *due process*, but if trial without a jury is legally provided for when permitted by the Constitution, in that instance, *due process* does not require jury trial. For cases in which the right of trial by jury is guaranteed see pages 111, 125, and 160.

"In a word, 'due process of law' to-day signifies 'reasonable law', in which sense it bestows upon the courts, and especially upon the Federal Courts, as final interpreter of the national constitution, a practically un-

defined range of supervision over legislation both state and national."
—*Cyclopedia of American Government*, Vol. I, p. 615.

"Due process of law, is law in its regular course of administration through courts of justice."—Story's *Commentaries*, Vol. III, pp. 264, 661;—18 *Howard* 272.

"Any legal proceeding enforced by public authority, whether sanctioned by age or custom, or newly devised in the discretion of the legislative power, in furtherance of the general public good, which regards and preserves these principles of liberty and justice."—110 *U. S.* 516.

"Due process of law in each particular case means, such an exercise of the powers of government as the settled maxims of the law permit and sanction, and under such safeguards for the protection of the individual rights as those maxims prescribe for the class of cases to which the one in question belongs."—Cooley's *Constitutional Limitations*, p. 441.

"This provision does not imply that all trials in state courts affecting the property of persons must be by jury." This depends to some extent upon the constitution of the respective states, except as limited by the United States Constitution.—92 *U. S.* 90.

2. Constitution of the United States, Amendment V.

Eminent domain means the right and authority of the government to take private property for public purposes upon the payment of a just compensation.

"The superior right existing in a sovereign government by which private property may in certain cases be taken or its use controlled for the public benefit, without regard to the wishes of the owner."—Bouvier's *Law Dictionary*, Vol. I, p. 657.

"Eminent domain is said with more precision to be the right of the nation or the state, or of those to whom the power has been lawfully delegated, to condemn private property to public use, upon paying to the owner a due compensation, to be ascertained according to law."—Bouvier's *Law Dictionary*, Vol. I, p. 651.

Just compensation is generally arrived at by those whose duty it is to secure the land for the government, by offering a good fair price for the land. If the owner of the land refuses to accept the offer, the land may be seized by the proper authority and the matter settled according to law. The law generally provides that a body of appraisers be appointed who appraise the value of the land and this amount is offered to the owner. If he refuses, the matter is carried to the court for determination. A jury is summoned to assess the value of the land and from this the owner may usually appeal, but the government cannot appeal; it must pay the appraised valuation or allow the owner to keep his property. It must be remembered that private property may only be taken by the government for public purposes.

Some purposes for which the government may take private property are: forts and arsenals, army posts, or public parks. It may take food supplies for use of the army or navy in time of war. It may take over the railroads for the benefit of the people of the Nation, etc. In all cases it must give just compensation.

ELEMENTARY QUESTIONS

1. What are the three things that every man, woman, and child cherishes?
2. What does the Constitution say about these three things?
3. What was the Bastile? The Tower of London?

4. Show how injustice was worked by confining people without due process of law.
5. What are some of the essentials of "due process of law"?
6. When can private property be taken by the government?
7. When the State wishes a piece of land, and the owner will not sell for a fair price, how is the matter adjusted?
9. What right for reconsideration has a person against whom a judgment has been rendered in a trial court?
9. How can the reasonable value of property be established or proven?
10. Suppose the President of the United States wished a certain piece of property upon which to build a summer home. Could the President secure the land? Give reasons.

ADVANCED QUESTIONS

A. What are some of the steps necessary to due process of law?
B. What would be the effect on people if life, liberty, or property could be taken without due process?
C. Discuss the process of condemning property.
D. Write a paper on the following:
   Evils of the Bastile and the Tower of London
   Why Military Courts Do Not Always Follow This Law
   The Different Purposes For Which Property May Be Taken For Public Use
   Why Ownership of Property Should Be Protected

XIV

CRIMINAL TRIALS

I hope no one here this morning will ever be arrested for a crime of any kind, and yet, as I have already explained to you, the innocent are sometimes brought before the court charged with a grave offense. Therefore you should be interested in the investigation of the truth of any charge that may be made against you, whether by a private individual or by a public officer.

I have already explained to you that in all grave offenses when a person is charged with a crime, he cannot be brought before the court for trial until the grand jury has investigated the facts and until they have returned an indictment, or written charge, to the court. Until this is done, the court has no power to proceed.

But now suppose that you have been arrested, suppose that a grand jury has investigated the charge against you, has heard witnesses, and has returned an indictment. You are then brought up before the court, and the indictment is read to you. This indictment I will explain to you more fully later. When the indictment is read you are then required to say whether you are "guilty" or "not guilty". If you have committed the crime charged, it may be advisable to plead guilty and ask for the mercy of the court in the punishment which he may impose. Courts usually temper justice with mercy. Courts will usually impose a lighter sentence when a guilty person pleads "guilty" and avoids the delay and expense of a trial. But, if you are innocent, you will plead "not guilty", and then the government, through its officers, will get ready for trial. You may not be tried right away, as it usually takes some time to investigate the facts and get the witnesses into court. As I will hereafter explain, you will be entitled to an attorney when the time comes for your trial, when you will have a chance to hear the witnesses offered by the prosecution, introduce your own witnesses, and, under our present law, testify yourself, tell your own story.

If you will walk into a court some day you will see the judge and over at one side twelve chairs for the jury. When your case is called for trial the first thing will be to select the twelve men who will be the jury in your case. I am not going to give the manner of selection at this time. This will be fully explained later. I wish now to impress upon you the fact that the Constitution expressly guards your rights by providing that you shall be entitled to have your case tried, not before a judge, but by a jury composed of men from the ordinary walks of life, laborers, merchants, farmers, people of all classes; men just like your fathers are. They are called. They hold up their right hands and take an oath to try your case fairly and justly and to make a finding according to the evidence which is brought before them.

The Constitution provides:

"In all criminal prosecutions, the accused shall enjoy the right to a speedy and public trial, by an impartial jury of the State and the district wherein the crime shall have been committed, which district shall have been previously ascertained by law."[1]

This is an absolute guaranty—a right which is given to you, given to each of you, to every man, woman, and child, young or old, regardless of color or creed. A trial without a jury would be a violation of your constitutional rights. Of course, there are a few minor offenses, misdemeanors, and violations of city ordinances, which are sometimes tried without a jury, but in all infamous crimes, for which life may be taken as punishment or for which a person may be sent to the penitentiary, every one is entitled to a trial before a jury.

Is not this a sacred right? Don't you think that it is wise to permit people to have their rights and wrongs determined by a body of plain, honest men? It removes any suggestion of the abuse of power by a person in a public position. It inspires confidence in those who are brought before the court for trial. If we cannot obtain justice before such a body of men, how can justice be obtained in this world?

I have already told you that in this country the people are not only the makers of the law but the enforcers of the law. It is in these jury trials where the people enforce the law.

Of course, the hearing before the jury is held in court. The judge presides. He directs the proceedings of the trial, sees that it is conducted in an orderly way, endeavors to prevent any falsehoods from getting before the jury, keeps away from the jury any hearsay or gossip, or expressions of prejudice, or other matters not founded on absolute knowledge and truth. But the jurors are the sole judges of what the truth is, and, when the case is closed, when the evidence has all been introduced and the attorneys have made their arguments and pleas, the members of the jury retire to a private room by themselves. There they discuss the evidence, come to some conclusion, make a finding of "guilty" or "not guilty", and bring in their finding in the form of a verdict.

Have you also observed that the constitutional protection of your liberty not only provides for a jury trial, but also provides that it shall be a "speedy" trial. That is, one charged with a crime cannot without his consent, be locked up for weeks and months and years, as has often occurred in other parts of the world. He is entitled to be tried just as soon as the case can be prepared for trial, in justice to both sides. Cases are often postponed for many months, but only by consent of the accused. A case not tried at the second term of court will usually be dismissed except when the defendant consents to the delay.

The Constitution also provides that it must be a public trial. Oh! how many men in the long ago have been tried and condemned in private, where only a few enemies were present, where one's friends and neighbors could not hear the charges or the evidence. In this country the doors of the court room must be open. Any one has a right to enter and listen to the proceedings. The public has a right to know what is being charged against the humblest citizen, and what the proceedings against him are. Thus is justice guarded.

Then the Constitution provides that the trial shall be before *"an impartial jury of the State and district wherein the crime shall have been committed."* This is important. We are not to be sent away among strangers to be tried. That is what they used to do long ago. That is one of the things which our forefathers complained of most bitterly. In the Declaration of Independence the colonies declared:

"He (the King of Great Britain) has combined with others to subject us to a jurisdiction foreign to our constititution, and unacknowledged by our laws; giving his Assent to their acts of pretended legislation . . . . for depriving us in many cases, of the benefits of Trial by Jury . . . . for transporting us beyond Seas to be tried for pretended offenses."

When the Constitution was adopted the people made up their minds that nothing of that kind should ever occur again in free America. They were so careful that they went so far as to provide that the district where a trial shall be held *"shall have been previously ascertained by law"*. That is to say, that the place of trial, the county or district where it shall be held, must be fixed by law before the crime is committed. The courts or the legislature of any State cannot, after a crime is committed, pass a law providing that such a crime shall be tried in a district then to be named. The law must fix this in advance of the commission of any offense. For instance, without such a constitutional provision, a person who committed a crime in the State of New York might be taken to California to be tried. This would not be American justice. The accused would have the right to point to the Constitution of his country and demand that he should be tried in New York, and any court which would not grant this right would not only violate the oath which every judge takes before he undertakes to perform the duties of such office, but his unlawful conduct would perhaps result in his impeachment. The proceedings would be reversed by a higher court, and the party would be granted a new trial at a place and in accordance with his constitutional privileges.

Isn't it wonderful how the little details which may affect one's liberty were so carefully considered away back there when they were planning the Nation and establishing the rules which would guard the rights of the people?

NOTES AND COMMENTS

1. Constitution of the United States, Amendment VI.

"A speedy trial is, it appears, one that is brought on without unreasonable delay for preparation; and a public trial is not necessarily one to which every one may obtain admission but one sufficiently free and open to allow the friends of the accused and others to watch the proceedings."—Emlin McClain, quoted in the *Cyclopedia of American Government.*

"Criminal prosecution is the means adopted to bring a supposed offender to justice and punishment by due course of law."

"The speedy trial to which a person charged with crime is entitled under the constitution is a trial at such a time, after the finding of the indictment, as shall afford the prosecution a reasonable opportunity, by the fair and honest exercise of reasonable diligence, to prepare for trial, and if the trial is delayed or postponed beyond such period, when there is a term of court at which the trial might be had, by reason of neglect of the prosecution in preparing for trial, such delay is a denial to the defendant of the right of a speedy trial, and in such case a person confined, upon application by *habeas corpus*, is entitled to a discharge from custody."—Bouvier's *Law Dictionary*, Vol. II, p. 1023.

Every jury is sworn to decide according to the evidence presented, guided by instructions in the law given by the judge. Juries are therefore held to be *impartial*.

The entire United States is divided into judicial districts, of which there are about ninety-two. These districts are found within the States as judicial districts do not cut State boundaries. Where the population is more sparse a Federal district comprises an entire State. Where the population is more dense a State may contain two or more districts. There are four United States District Court districts in the State of New York, two in Iowa, and only one in Nevada, and some other western States.

Congress may by legislative act lay out Federal court districts. These districts were first established in the Federal Judiciary Act of 1789. As the population increases Congress may increase the number of districts.

ELEMENTARY QUESTIONS

1. Why should all of us be interested in a trial?
2. Describe a court room scene.
3. Why is trial by jury a sacred right? What would it be like if we did not have this right?
4. How are jurors selected in your State?
5. Why is the trial to be held in the vicinity where the crime was committed? What would be the dangers of taking it far away?
6. Why should the jury be impartial?
7. If the accused person is guilty, why is it advisable to plead guilty?
8. Why is it impracticable to hold a trial immediately after the arrest of the accused person?
9. What is the first step in the actual trial?
10. After a jury is selected, what is required of them before the trial commences?
11. Why is a speedy trial essential to justice?
12. Why is it important that the trial should be public?
13. State some offenses that are sometimes tried without a jury.

ADVANCED QUESTIONS

A. Can the judge declare an accused man guilty?
B. How is trial by jury an evidence of the rule of the people?
C. Show how this benefits the poor man and the rich man equally.
D. Why are some trials delayed for many months?
E. What is the importance of the clause "shall have been previously ascertained by law"?
F. Discuss the relative role of jury and judge in a trial.
G. Write a paper on the following:
   The Method of Selecting Jurors in Your State
   Delay in Trial
   The Injustice of Remote Trials
   Trial by Jury vs. Trial by a Judge
   The Procedure of a Trial From Beginning to End

XV

THE INDICTMENT

DEFENDANT MUST BE INFORMED CONCERNING THE ACCUSATION AGAINST HIM

Now, my friends, in order to understand more fully the value of our constitutional rights, let us again imagine ourselves in a place of danger, danger of our liberty or of our life, and let us recall how carefully we have been guarded. To the poorest tramp, or the richest millionaire, the same rules apply. Innocent persons may be accused of crimes; they may be arrested, but they cannot be brought into court and put upon trial until they are fully advised of the charge against them.

The Constitution provides:

"In all criminal prosecutions, the accused shall . . . . be informed of the nature and cause of the accusation".[1]

This is the first step in bringing a person to trial. He does not go blindly. He must be informed "of the nature and cause" of the charge against him. He must be given full knowledge of the crime which it is claimed he committed. *How is this done?* Well, we have to consider the constitutional provision that one cannot be put upon trial for an infamous crime *"unless on a presentment or indictment of a Grand Jury"*. What this constitutional provision means is, that a grand jury shall hear and consider the evidence and, if satisfied that a person shall be tried, they shall draw up a writing called an "indictment", which they shall return publicly in court. This indictment is a brief statement by which the grand jury makes a charge against the person named of having committed a certain offense, and the indictment must state not only the name of the offense, but the manner, briefly stated, in which the grand jury claims the offense was committed.

So that under this constitutional guaranty the person accused knows what he is to be tried for. This enables him to prepare for his defense. When his attorney is consulted he examines a copy of the indictment. He sees what is charged in it. He then talks over with the accused the facts and circumstances with relation to the crime charged. He then makes proper inquiry. If possible he secures witnesses with relation to the charge and thus is enabled to come into court ready to hear the evidence offered by the prosecution and ready to introduce witnesses to contradict or explain the testimony introduced by the prosecution.

So you see how valuable this right is. One may proceed intelligently, with full light upon the alleged transaction. He is not required to stumble in the darkness, perhaps to tumble into a pitfall. Without such a provision you can see how helpless an innocent person might be if brought suddenly before the court for trial for an offense which he never committed. If he were not first advised of the nature of the charge and the circumstances he might be helpless. You know evidence is brought before the court by witnesses who are called by the attorneys for the prosecution and for the accused. These witnesses take oath to tell the truth. But, unfortunately, witnesses do not always tell the truth. They sometimes commit perjury. One must be ready to meet false testimony. By the constitutional guaranty requiring that the accusation be in writing, stating the crime and its nature, one can be prepared. In many of the States still greater precaution is taken to guard against any possible wrong, by requiring not only an indictment but also requiring that there shall be furnished to the person accused the names of witnesses and a brief statement of the evidence which the prosecution expects to offer, this to be furnished before the trial commences so that the defendant may get ready to meet it.

Did you ever go into a court when a man was upon trial for a grave offense? You should do so. Everyone should do so. But you should go there with the proper spirit, not for amusement, not to criticise, but with a full realization of the great human drama there being enacted. There at or near the trial table you will see the defendant, the man who is being tried. He may be a stranger. He may be poor. He may possibly be wicked, but he is a human being; and no matter what faults he may have he is an American citizen, and under the Constitution of our country he cannot be convicted until proven guilty of the particular crime charged in the indictment. He sits there while witnesses are telling their stories. You will see him watching the jury. Occasionally he looks at the judge. But he knows that no matter what the judge may think, he cannot find him guilty. The jury and the jury alone can convict.

It is a solemn proceeding, though the lawyers may at times appear to use trifling words in their discussions. The prisoner looks through the court room window. Outside the sun is shining, the birds are singing, and the breezes sway the branches of the green trees. Everything seems to suggest liberty and freedom. At no time is liberty so sweet as when it is in danger. The prisoner realizes that in a few days the trial will be ended and the verdict of the jury will determine whether he shall go out of the court room to freedom or to prison.

To-day it is the stranger who is on trial. To-morrow it may be someone who is near and dear to you. If such misfortune should come, then you will fully realize what a wonderful blessing it is that under our Constitution everyone is assured of a fair trial, that a person can only be tried for the specific offense stated in the indictment, and that a verdict of guilty can only be rendered when the evidence is strong enough to convince the jury of guilt beyond a reasonable doubt.

NOTES AND COMMENTS

1. Constitution of the United States, Amendment VI.

If one is not given a preliminary hearing shortly after his arrest, the right to a writ of *habeas corpus* (defined in another chapter), gives the accused an opportunity to know the exact nature of the charge against him and why he is held or detained in prison. Then he is faced by his accusers in court and hears the charge against him. In all criminal cases the accused is privileged to be present throughout the entire trial, in fact he is required to be present during the trial.

In early England, and in many other European countries in early times, the accused person was not even permitted to know the reason for his imprisonment, and furthermore was tried in court and found guilty without hearing the evidence or knowing who testified in court.

The right of trial upon indictment of a grand jury, and the privilege of confronting one's accusers in court, having witnesses in one's behalf, and having an attorney to defend one accused, is not yet allowed in certain parts of Russia and perhaps other countries in Europe and Asia. These privileges have been the recognized right of all people in the United States since our glorious Constitution was adopted and became the fundamental law of our country in 1789.

Teachers of civics in our schools ought to ask permission of the judge to take their classes to visit a session of the court. The judge is able to inform the teacher as to when certain cases of most value to pupils and other persons are to be tried. The trial of certain kinds of cases brings out many fundamental facts of rights and duties of citizenship that boys and girls, as well as many adult persons, ought to know.

"The accused is of all men the most miserable, unless the law gives him an equal chance to defend himself. Time was when the courts could hear privately the witnesses against the prisoner, and then call him into court to answer charges, which he never had heard of, made upon the testimony of witnesses he never had seen, without any legal means of compelling his own witnesses to come to court to testify for him and without any lawyer to speak for him against the trained counsel for the government. Many of these abuses had been weeded out before the Constitution was adopted."—Bacon's *American Plan of Government*, p. 272.

"Almost all the reform needed to make criminal procedure humane and just, has been incorporated into the constitutions and laws of the states during the first era of independence; but the people of the United States had no such safeguards."—Bacon's *American Plan of Government*, p. 273.

"The charge to be answered by the defendant on trial in a criminal court must be clear, explicit, and definite. The prosecution has no right to compel the accused to show that he is a good member of society."— 7 *Peters Rep.* 138.

ELEMENTARY QUESTIONS

1. Restate the guaranties that every man has before being brought to trial.
2. Why should the accused be informed of the nature of the accusation?
3. What would be the result if he were not so informed?
4. Why is it necessary that this accusation be put in writing?
5. Why is this important to everybody?

ADVANCED QUESTIONS

A. Illustrate the dangers of secret charges.
B. What chance has a person with malicious and secret gossip?
C. Upon a trial can evidence of hearsay or gossip be offered to prove guilt?
D. When a person makes a charge against a person and says, "Don't tell anyone that I said this", what is the effect?
E. Tell some of the dangers and injustices of slander.
F. What is the first step in bringing an accused person to trial?
G. Is it sufficient to charge the defendant with having committed murder without any further explanation? Give reasons.
H. What is required of a witness before he is examined?
I. What is perjury?
J. Why is a trial a solemn proceeding?
K. How strong must the evidence be in order that a person may be found guilty?
L. Write a paper on the following:
   The Need of a Public and Written Charge
   The Danger of the Secret Slander
   How An Accused Person Prepares For His Trial
   A Visit to a Court in Session

XVI

GUARDING RIGHTS IN COURT

CONFRONTED BY WITNESSES—COMPULSORY PROCESS—AID OF COUNSEL—JURY IN CIVIL TRIAL

I am sure that no one until he has studied the Constitution, no one certainly who is not a trained lawyer, will realize the many safeguards necessary to protect persons who may be wrongfully accused of a crime; but the framers of the Constitution knew the dangers from the sad experiences of innocent men and women who had been sacrificed by tyrants who had but little regard for human life or for human liberty.

Of course you now understand that in case an indictment is returned by the grand jury, the person accused comes into court, or is brought in, and enters his plea of "guilty" or of "not guilty". If he pleads "not guilty" a jury is brought together, "empanelled", as it is called, and they are sworn to hear the evidence, and decide the case according to the evidence.

But in these grave criminal trials, in order that the truth may prevail, every accused person is given the right to be confronted by the witnesses against him. The Constitution provides:

"In all criminal prosecutions, the accused shall . . . . be confronted with the witnesses against him".[1]

What does this mean? It means that the government, the prosecution, cannot prove guilt by witnesses who are not present in court where the defendant can see them, where they may be cross examined by counsel, where the jury may observe them, and study their conduct and demeanor, because this often helps in determining whether a person is telling the truth or a falsehood.

In ordinary trials where property alone is involved, a

witness may live in another State or at some great distance from the place of trial. Witnesses cannot be brought a long distance in those cases. In some States they cannot be compelled to attend a distance of more than seventy miles. In other States, not more than one hundred miles; so that to get their testimony, the parties take their depositions. This means that instead of bringing the witness into court, the parties obtain an order by which they can go to the place where the witness is. There he is sworn before a commissioner, or a notary public, examined, and his testimony is taken in writing. The testimony is returned to the court where the trial is to be held, and is then read to the court or the jury upon the trial.

But in the trial of a person accused of a crime, depositions cannot be used against him. Statements of witnesses in writing, or in any other form, cannot be used by the prosecution. The witnesses must be physically in court before the accused, and there orally testify, and the defendant must have the right to cross examine them.

But to give the accused person every possible aid in enabling him to have the truth brought before the court and jury, he may take the depositions of witnesses in his own behalf. That is, the prosecution—the State or the Nation accusing a man of a crime—must prove the truth of the accusation by witnesses personally in court confronting the defendant, but the defendant is given the privilege of taking the testimony of witnesses at a distance, in the form of depositions which are read to the jury.

This provision of the Constitution may be very important to an innocent person sometimes. The importance of it may never appear to us until unfortunately we be wrongfully accused of a crime, and our life or liberty in danger.

Then the Constitution further provides:

"In all criminal prosecutions, the accused shall enjoy the

right . . . . to have compulsory process for obtaining witnesses in his favor".[2]

This is also very important. "Compulsory process" means an order of the court, commonly called "subpoena", which is served upon witnesses by the marshal, or the sheriff, or other authorized person, commanding them to appear in court for examination before the court and jury as to the truth of matters involved in the accusation against a person on trial.

Here I wish you to recall the unfortunate fact that every little while somebody is complaining about our government as "a rich man's government". It is often claimed that the poor have no chance for justice. The truth is that the rich and the poor stand equal in the courts. In creating the Constitution, it is known of course that someone might be brought before the court who was poor, without money, possibly without friends. He might be innocent, but in order that his innocence might be established it would be necessary for him to have witnesses who might live many miles away, who would not come into court to testify of their own free will. Therefore, there was inserted in the Constitution this provision, that every defendant shall have the right to compulsory process, commanding witnesses to appear, and there is no one so poor that he cannot have this privilege, because the United States—and in most of the States we have a like provision—not only issues subpoenas and compels the officers to serve them, but it pays the expense of serving, and pays the witness fees and mileage, so that the poor man has all of the rights in getting the truth before the court and jury that the richest may have.

Furthermore, in the same American spirit, when persons accused of an offense are too poor to employ counsel, the government will furnish counsel. The Constitution provides:

"In all criminal prosecutions, the accused shall . . . .
have the Assistance of Counsel for his defence."[3]

There is no person so poor, or obscure, or friendless, that when he is charged with a crime which might affect his liberty or his life, he shall not have the right to a full, fair trial. Not only are his witnesses produced and paid by the government, but an attorney is appointed by the government to represent him, and help him establish his innocence.

This is a wonderful illustration of the paternal care which is manifested for those who may be unfortunate, and this is all because under our Constitution, liberty is a sacred thing, and it shall not be taken away except in punishment for a crime which has been proven in open court in a public trial before a jury, where the party has been confronted with the witnesses against him, where he has had a chance to furnish witnesses in his behalf and the aid of counsel in his trial.

Then the people who brought the Constitution into being, feeling that so far as practicable they should have control of the enforcement of law not only in criminal cases, but in civil cases, included a guaranty in the Constitution that:

"In suits at common law, where the value in controversy
shall exceed twenty dollars, the right of trial by jury shall
be preserved".[4]

Of course there is often more or less controversy about property of small value, where the expense and delay of jury trials might possibly be oppressive, but in any case involving more than twenty dollars in value, triable under the common law, which includes practically all cases except those peculiar cases triable in Chancery, or in Courts of Equity, the parties are entitled to a trial by jury. That is, instead of introducing their evidence and having the judge decide what the truth is between them, the parties are entitled to have a jury of men from the ordinary occupations of life hear the evidence and say from the evidence what is the truth.

And furthermore, the people provided in the Constitution that:

"No fact tried by a jury shall be otherwise re-examined in any Court of the United States, than according to the rules of the common law."[5]

Here again is the right to a jury trial, and the benefit of a jury trial, and to a trial according to the established rules and precedents of the common law courts carefully preserved.

Now my friends, I know that there is much confusion in your minds about trials in court. I do not expect you to know all about trials. We are studying the guaranties of the Constitution so that we shall learn human rights—our rights —under the Constitution. I am talking to you about the safeguards of the Constitution so you shall know your rights, especially so that you will always venerate the Constitution which guards your rights, and defend it against those who may assail it. But I do want you to have a clear idea of what a trial in court is. I want you to know the purpose of the long days of examination of witnesses, the objections of the attorneys to certain questions asked, the rulings of the court, and the arguments of counsel.

The main purpose, aim, and object of every lawsuit, as trials are usually termed by people who are not lawyers, *is to find the truth.* The proceedings in court in every lawsuit are a continuous search for the truth. If in disputes we could agree to what the truth is, there would be few lawsuits to try.

A lawsuit only arises where there is a dispute to settle. If people agreed about their rights there would be little need of courts. In criminal cases, the government through the grand jury charges by indictment that a man committed a certain crime. The government says the man did it. He denies it by a plea of not guilty. He says he did not. The trial before the petit jury is merely a search for the truth about the charge. *What is the truth about the matter in dispute,* that is all that is involved in an ordinary lawsuit.

Picture two boys in a dispute about which owns a ball. One positively asserts that it is his, that his father bought it and gave it to him. The other is just as sure that it is his. He says that his brother gave it to him. They quarrel so excitedly that a neighbor coming across the street asks the cause of the trouble. They tell him their claims and ask him to decide. One boy points out a rough spot on the ball which he insists was caused by a blow from his bat while he was playing in his own yard. The other says that his brother gave him a ball with red and white stitches. The neighbor, after hearing these and many other claims, decides the case, giving the ball to the boy whom he finds to be the owner.

In this we have every element of a lawsuit. The dispute, the court (the neighbor), the witnesses (the boys), and the judgment based upon what the neighbor finds to be the truth from the evidence before him. That is all that any court or jury can do, but under the Constitution in cases involving life or liberty every possible safeguard is provided so that the truth may be found, so that justice may be done.

NOTES AND COMMENTS

1. Constitution of the United States, Amendment VI.

"In judicial procedure a witness is one who is duly called upon to testify under oath as to matters within his knowledge. By rules of procedure some persons are disqualified from testifying on account of want of mental capacity as, for instance, idiots, insane persons, and infants who have not attained the age of discretion. Others who are qualified to testify may be of such character that their testimony is not entitled to the weight which should be given to some other witness. Furthermore, a witness may be so related to the subject matter or to the parties as that in the particular case his testimony should not be received, or should be received under limitations as to its credibility and weight. And finally the competency of testimony offered is regulated by rules of evidence fixed by law."

"Under constitutional guaranties of religious freedom, the religious belief of a witness cannot be made a ground for his disqualification to testify."

"As to criminal prosecution, it is usually provided in state constitutions as it is in the Fifth and Sixth Amendments to the Federal Constitution that the accused shall not be compelled to be a witness against himself and that he has a right to be confronted with the witnesses against him and to have compulsory process for obtaining witnesses in his favor. These are privileges which the accused may waive."—Emlin McClain, quoted in *Cyclopedia of American Government*, Vol. III, p. 693.

2. "Compulsory process is the means of compelling a witness to appear before the court at the time of trial and, under oath, tell what he knows about the matter under consideration."—Bouvier's *Law Dictionary*, Vol. II, p. 766.

A *subpoena* is an order issued in a court and given to a sheriff or other executive officer, to be served upon or read to a witness, compelling him to appear before the court at the time stated. He must lay aside all pretenses and excuses, and appear before the court or the magistrate at the time and place named in the subpoena, under a penalty therein cited for failure to appear. His failure to obey the order of the court, or subpoena, is known as *contempt*. Contempt is punishable in Federal courts, and in most States by the order of the judge, and is not subject to jury trial. (Oklahoma is an exception.)

3. "At common law a prisoner was not allowed counsel. In England this right was not granted in all cases before 1836."—*Cyclopedia of American Government*, Vol. I, p. 487.

The United States was the earliest of nations to not only permit every person accused of crime and tried before a court to have counsel, but to furnish counsel for every person who was not himself able to get counsel or able to pay for counsel.

4. Constitution of the United States, Amendment VII.

"Common Law is that system of law or form of the science of jurisprudence which has prevailed in England and in the United States, in contradistinction from other great systems, such as Roman or civil law."—Bouvier's *Law Dictionary*, Vol. I, p. 370.

"Common law is used to distinguish the body of rules and of remedies administered by courts of law, technically so called, in contradistinction to those of equity administered by courts of chancery, and to the canon law, administered by ecclesiastical courts."—Bouvier's *Law Dictionary*, Vol. I, p. 370.

5. Constitution of the United States, Amendment VII.

"A jury is a body of men sworn to declare the *facts* of a case as they are proven from the evidence placed before them."—Bouvier's *Law Dictionary*.

The definition of a jury explains why the facts of a case are not open for re-examination after being declared by a jury. It is because a jury meets in a court in the place where the offense has been committed, and is therefore better able to know the whole truth, and to determine what the facts really are than would be possible for any other body of men who did not have such means of knowing. A higher court in reviewing a case on an appeal cannot usually go behind the facts as declared by a jury.

ELEMENTARY QUESTIONS

1. Why should all witnesses for the prosecution speak in the actual presence of the accused?
2. Why should the accused be allowed to have testimony in his favor submitted in writing?
3. In what cases is written testimony ordinarily admitted?
4. What is compulsory process?
5. In what ways does the Constitution aid the poor man?
6. In what cases may there be a trial without a jury?
7. What is the main purpose of any lawsuit?
8. What is meant by cross-examination of a witness?

ADVANCED QUESTIONS

A. In what way do these provisions sustain the fact that our government is a democracy?
B. Is a person more likely to commit perjury when not actually facing the person accused? Give reasons.
C. What is the provision of the Constitution as to "compulsory process"? Explain the importance of this right.
D. Explain the provision of the Constitution as to the right to have counsel.
E. Show how compulsory process and free counsel help the poor man.
F. Why is jury trial omitted in small controversies?
G. What is a "civil" case?
H. Write a paper on the following:
   How Perjury is Detected
   Oral and Written Testimony
   How the Poor Man is Protected
   The Purpose of a Trial in Court
   The Story of a Tramp Without Money, Accused of an Offense:
      How the Constitution Helps Him

XVII

PUNISHMENT

PROHIBITION OF EXCESSIVE BAIL OR FINES, CRUEL OR UNUSUAL PUNISHMENTS, AND INVOLUNTARY SERVITUDE

Before we finish, I want you to have in your mind a clear conception of the way in which a person accused of an offense is brought before the court, tried, and convicted or acquitted.

I have already explained that the first step is the arrest of the suspected person.[1] Again put yourself in the place of the suspected person.

You are arrested. It is the duty of the officer making the arrest to bring you into a court, but this is not generally to a trial court. A person is generally brought before what is called a committing magistrate, a justice of the peace or commissioner—some person having authority to issue warrants of arrest. You may be far from home and friends when you are arrested. You may be entirely unacquainted in the neighborhood. The government is not ready to proceed to your trial. Witnesses must be summoned, not only for the government, but if you have witnesses you desire to use, they must be brought in.

The general rule is to set the case for hearing—a "preliminary hearing" in a day or two, or a week possibly. You must therefore wait until this time comes. What are you going to do? Must you go to jail until they get ready to have the hearing? No, you are entitled to bail; that is, you are entitled to be discharged upon a bond fixed by the magistrate, commissioner, or judge. There are usually only two offenses which are not, as the saying is, bailable—murder and treason. Usually where murder or treason is charged, the person is not admitted to bail. He is locked up in a cell to await trial; but as a general rule, when a person is arrested his bail is fixed—that is, the amount of the bond which he must file in order to be discharged pending the trial. For instance, if it were a charge of stealing a bicycle, the court might fix the bail at $500 or $1000. That would mean that if he would file a bond, with sureties, conditioned that in case he did not appear for hearing—that he should run away, for instance—the sureties would pay into the court the amount of the bond. Mostly any person of fair standing in a community can secure some friends who will sign such a bond, so that he may have his liberty until the trial.

But the framers of the Constitution, again anxious about the liberties of the people, provided:

"Excessive bail shall not be required".[2]

There were many instances in the olden days where bail was purposely fixed so high—so far beyond all reason in view of the nature of the offense that the party could not furnish the bail, the purpose being to compel the party to remain in prison. Our Constitution guarantees to every individual that the amount of bail fixed shall be reasonable in view of the nature of the offense and if it is not reasonable, the person arrested may have the matter brought before the court, who will make full inquiry, and reduce the amount of the bail if found to be too large.

All through these guaranties of the Constitution, all through these provisions guarding the sacred rights of every person, you will see that the effort is that justice shall be done, not injustice; that right shall prevail, not wrong. That no one shall be kept in prison, deprived of his liberty, unless absolutely necessary in the interest of justice.

Then after a trial, if a person is found guilty, the Constitution again guards the rights even of the guilty, by providing:

"Excessive fines (shall not be) imposed, nor cruel and unusual punishments inflicted."[3]

When this constitutional guaranty was written persons then living could recall without doubt the barbarous punishments which had been imposed in civilized countries even for light offenses. Common hanging was not regarded as sufficient punishment. "Hanged, drawn and quartered" was often heard in the courts of countries which had been left behind. It was nothing uncommon to see persons upon the roadside in England left hanging to the gibbet for long periods of time where the people could see them as a warning. It was not uncommon in those times to have a penalty of death imposed for the offense of stealing.

It is almost impossible to read of the punishments of the olden days, even under decrees of courts, without a shudder. Therefore, every one in America should be filled with gratitude that in the adoption of our Constitution these excessive cruelties were forever ended.

We have in this country the death penalty only for the most grave offenses, and it is seldom imposed. Imprisonment is generally regarded as just and sufficient. I might spend an hour if we had time, telling you something of the horrible dungeons which served as prisons in the olden days, into which God's sunlight seldom entered; of the chains the prisoners had to wear; of the starvation; yes, and of the lash —inhumanities which one can scarcely conceive, and which can never disgrace the civilization of America.

Again, carefully guarding the rights and liberties of the people we find:

"Neither slavery nor involuntary servitude, except as a punishment for crime whereof the party shall have been duly

convicted, shall exist within the United States, or any place subject to their jurisdiction."[4]

This is not a part of the original Constitution. It was adopted after the war had driven slavery from our shores. The spirit of America has from the beginning been exerted in enlarging the rights of human beings. Slavery existed before the adoption of the Constitution, and so strongly was it intrenched at that time in some of the colonies that it was impossible then to wipe it out.

But it did not belong in America, and the time came when the American people, after a long bitter war, crushed the slave power, and swept from our shores the last vestige of involuntary servitude. That it might not be renewed, the people amended the Constitution so as forever to bar slavery or involuntary servitude except as men might be put in prison in punishment for crime after a full, fair trial.

Did you ever read of the debtor's prison? It used to be in nearly every country in the world, that men who were merely unfortunate, who got in debt and who could not pay when the debt was due were sent to prison, and kept there sometimes for long periods. It was most cruel, because in many instances the persons were honest. They wanted to pay their debts, but sickness came, or floods, or fire, or other misfortune, and when the time came they were unable to pay and thus they lost their liberty.

In those olden days, men were not only imprisoned, but in some countries they were compelled to labor for the person whom they owed. They were compelled to be slaves.

But at last we have reached a stage in America, where no one may be compelled to work for another, unless by his own free will, except under conviction of a crime where the State may compel prisoners to work for some one in order to help pay the expense of maintaining them.

The old debtor's prison is gone. No one in this country

can now be imprisoned for an ordinary debt. There are a few States in which a person may be imprisoned for debts arising in fraud, but for an ordinary contract debt, mere inability to pay, no one in America can now be compelled to submit to imprisonment.

I wish sometime you would think seriously about what America has done for the poor. In the olden days they had few if any rights; but to-day in America, while by law we cannot prevent sickness nor sorrow, or other misfortune, we can and we do guard the liberty of the poorest and the most unfortunate. In fact many laws have been enacted which give to the poor special privileges which are denied to those who have property or money.

For instance in nearly every State there are what are called exemptions for a person who is the head of a family, which protect him even in the possession of a limited amount of property which his creditors cannot take away from him in payment of a debt. In most of the States laborers may hold the earnings of a certain period, for instance ninety days, for support of themselves and their families, which no one can touch, which no officers and no court can seize in payment of a debt. Also they are protected in their household goods, their clothing for themselves and their families, and in many other ways.

The farmer who may be heavily in debt is protected for himself and his family by having exempted to him a team of horses, harness and wagon, machinery, farm utensils, and food and clothing for the family.

I have not time to relate all that has been done by America in sympathetic aid of the poor and the unfortunate. No other country in the world has given such consideration to the poor as has America.

We hear much talk of social injustice, that the poor man has no chance. The truth is that more has been done in

America during the past twenty-five years to provide justice for the poor and unfortunate and for those who toil, than was done in any other country of the world during the last one thousand years. The spirit of America is right. The people have the power. They are right at heart. The only weakness in America is the failure of many thousands of our men and women to take an active interest in the affairs of government. Hundreds of thousands, yes millions, of our voters fail to go to the polls on election day to vote. They do not seem to feel any gratitude for the privilege of living in a free country where liberty is guarded by written guaranties of a Constitution which cannot be changed, except by the will of the people themselves.

NOTES AND COMMENTS

1. In ordinary instances arrests may be made only by officers of the law upon warrants issued by a magistrate. Any officer may, however, upon his own cognizance of a crime being committed, arrest the person or persons without warrant. If such authority were not given to officers of the law, many persons violating law would be able to escape before a warrant could be issued. Furthermore, under the laws of some States, any person who sees a crime committed is legally required to pursue and arrest the offending person and may himself be punished if he refuses to act. Sheriffs and other officers of the peace may call upon and require other persons to assist in the pursuit and capture of fleeing criminals.

2. Constitution of the United States, Amendment VIII.
In criminal actions the matter of bail is determined by statute. Bail is often denied to those accused of committing serious crimes.

The term *bail* is used to designate a person who becomes a surety for the appearance of the defendant in court at the time called for. But in modern usage the term *bail* means the amount of money pledged by another person for the appearance of the defendant. If the defendant fails to appear the person going his bail must pay the stipulated amount into the court. The payment of the bail does not, however, relieve the delinquent defendant of further punishment. He may be again seized and punished as according to the charge, and furthermore may be given additional punishment for "jumping" his bail.

"The defendant usually binds himself as principal with two sureties; but sometimes the bail alone binds himself as principal, and sometimes one surety is accepted by the sheriff. The bail bond may be said to stand in the place of the defendant as far as the sheriff is concerned, and if properly taken, furnishes the sheriff a complete answer to the requirement of the writ, requiring him to take and produce the body of the defendant."—Bouvier's *Law Dictionary*, Vol. I, p. 211.

3. United States Constitution, Amendment VIII.

"The amount of fine is frequently left to the discretion of the court, who ought to proportion the fine to the offense."—Cooley's *Constitutional Limitations*, p. 377.

"The object of punishment is to reform the offender, to deter him and others from committing like offenses, and to protect society." "A state may provide a severer punishment for a second than for a first offense providing it is dealt out to all alike."—159 *U. S.* 673.

"Punishments are cruel when they involve torture or a lingering death; but the punishment of death is not cruel, within the meaning of that word as used in the Constitution."—136 *U. S.* 436.

A warden of a State penitentiary was recently found guilty of inflicting cruel punishment because he punished a convict by suspending his body from chains placed around his wrists.

The British Museum contains several machines of torture used to punish criminals in early days. One is a machine in the form of a hollow case fitting a human form. This case is filled with sharp spikes driven through from the outside. The machine was so constructed that when a victim was placed inside, the sides could be gradually turned up to fit the body and press these spikes into the body of the victim so as to produce death.

Another machine is constructed much as a cross in form of the letter X. The victim was fastened in such manner as to bind his wrists and ankles to the ends of the bars. A horse was then hitched to either his arms or legs and they were torn from the body.

Many States in the United States have now adopted electrocution as the means of inflicting the death penalty because it is believed to be the most humane way.

4. Constitution of the United States, Amendment XIII, Sec. 1.

This amendment was submitted to the States by resolution of Congress in 1865 and by proclamation of the President of December 18th of that year was declared to have received the approval of the requisite number of States.

So far as the abolition of slavery is involved there has been no question as to the effect of the amendment, but as to what constitutes involuntary servitude important questions have arisen. While the primary object of the amendment was to free the colored race, the general purpose was to render impossible the existence within the jurisdiction of the United States of any legal or social institution imposing involuntary labor on any class of persons. The introduction here of the peonage system prevalent in Mexico, the coolie system of China, or the padrone system of Italy fall within the prohibition.

The amendment permits imprisonment and also involuntary servitude as a penalty for failure to pay a fine imposed as a punishment. Moreover the services of persons imprisoned for crime belong to the State and may be leased, subject of course to humanitarian regulations as to the method in which such services may be employed.

Under the enforcement clause Congress has legislated against peonage, that is, a condition of enforced servitude by which the servitor is restrained of his liberty and compelled to labor in liquidation of some contract, debt, or obligation. But without such legislation, State statutes imposing imprisonment or servitude for non-performance of contractual obligations are invalid as in conflict with the provisions of the amendment.—Emlin McClain, in the *Cyclopedia of American Government*, Vol. III, p. 536.

In the early days many of the American colonies permitted imprisonment for debt, and one of the greatest patriots and philanthropists of colonial times, Robert Morris, was imprisoned for debt by the State of Pennsylvania.

ELEMENTARY QUESTIONS

1. After a person is arrested where is he generally taken by the officer?
2. If the hearing is postponed, what is generally done with him in the meantime?
3. What is bail?
4. What offenses are not bailable?
5. What is the constitutional guaranty as to bail?
6. Why should excessive bail be prohibited? What would be the injustice of this practice?
7. What happens when a person "out on bail" fails to appear in court at the time set? Is he relieved of further punishment?
8. If a magistrate fixes excessive bail, what may the accused person do in order to have it reduced?
9. Name some cruel and unusual punishments?
10. When was slavery in America abolished?
11. What was a debtor's prison?
12. How does America protect the poor? Can a debtor be put in prison for failing to pay ordinary debts?
13. What is meant by "exemptions" in relation to property and debts?

ADVANCED QUESTIONS

A. Explain the injustice of requiring excessive bail?
B. When a judge determines the amount of bail, what factors does he consider?
C. What is the purpose of punishment?
D. Discuss the movement for prison reform.
E. What is the purpose of the bankruptcy law?
F. Write a paper on:
   Cruel and Unusual Punishments
   Punishment and Crime in the United States
   How America Protects the Poor Man
   The Reformatory Versus the Penitentiary

XVIII

EQUAL RIGHTS OF CITIZENS

ALL CITIZENS ENTITLED TO EQUAL PRIVILEGES AND IMMUNITIES—RIGHT TO VOTE NOT ABRIDGED

The great achievement in American government was the establishment of a Nation composed of independent and sovereign States. It was not an easy matter to bring all these States together as one government, so that there would be harmony and unity; but the framers of the Constitution succeeded in a wonderful way in adopting rules and regulations—the Constitution—which made this the most powerful and the most peaceful Nation in the world.[1]

Only once has there been any serious question between the States, and the Civil War settled that forever. Following the war, to bind the States more firmly together by the establishment of the rights of citizens of the various States, an amendment to the Constitution was adopted in 1868, by the people of the Nation, which is as follows:

"All persons born or naturalized in the United States, and subject to the jurisdiction thereof, are citizens of the United States and of the State wherein they reside. No State shall make or enforce any law which shall abridge the privileges or immunities of citizens of the United States; nor shall any State deprive any person of life, liberty, or property without due process of law; nor deny to any person within its jurisdiction the equal protection of the laws."[2]

This portion of our Constitution establishes the citizenship of every person born or naturalized in the United States, and guarantees the rights of such citizens, not only in the State where he lives, but in any State. No State has the power, since the adoption of this amendment, to make or enforce any law which shall abridge the privileges, rights, or immunities of citizens, no matter in what State they may make their home.

By this amendment all States are prohibited from enacting any law, or permitting any procedure of their courts, which shall "deprive any person of life, liberty, or property, without due process of law".

You will recall that immediately after the adoption and approval of the original Constitution there were ten amendments adopted which became effective in 1791, in one of which it was provided that no person "shall be deprived of life, liberty or property, without due process of law". This forever barred the United States government from depriving the humblest citizen of his life, his liberty, or his property, except through the regular processes of the law which we have heretofore considered; and by the amendment of 1868 the same restriction was placed upon every State in the Union, thus completing the guaranty to every man, woman, and child, that life, liberty, and property would be safe and sacred. No power exists in the State or Nation by which life, liberty, or property may be interfered with, except through the tribunals established by the people themselves to hear and determine in a judicial way after proper notice with full opportunity to be heard in a public trial.

No secret schemes can be devised which will interfere with the rights of the humblest citizen, no power can be created strong enough wrongfully to invade the right to life, liberty, and property. These guaranties, being written into the Constitution, will stand forever, unless the people by their own choice shall throw away these great guaranties and destroy these great blessings.

Then following the Civil War, the people of America adopted the following as part of the Constitution of the United States:

"The right of citizens of the United States to vote shall not be denied or abridged by the United States or by any State on account of race, color, or previous condition of servitude."[3]

You remember the Emancipation Proclamation by President Lincoln which struck the chains from the limbs of men and women and children who had been slaves for generations. They were human beings, though of the colored race. They were lifted from the position of slavery to the dignity of citizenship, and clothed with power to help in the government of their country by being given the privilege of going to the ballot box to vote. To establish this right and protect this privilege for all time, this amendment to the Constitution was adopted by the people of the United States. It was a bold thing to do, to clothe a subject race which had little opportunity for education with the rights of citizenship. No nation in the world ever before attempted such a wonderful and radical experiment; but the people of America, having real confidence in human beings, regardless of color, race, or creed, assumed the responsibility of admitting the former slaves as part of the power of government in this country.

Of course you realize that the value of a citizen to his country, when it comes to voting and making laws, depends upon his knowledge of public affairs, and his confidence in his government; and therefore education is absolutely necessary to real service to one's country. That is one of the big objects of education—to qualify persons for full citizenship.[4]

Too many of us consider the right to vote simply as a privilege to help some neighbor to be elected to some public office. This view is all wrong. Our country is first, and we never should help a neighbor to be elected to an office unless that neighbor can help to make this a better government.[5]

When we elect any one, we are selecting a servant to represent us, to act for us. Therefore great care should be exercised in selection. We must inquire not only whether the person is good and virtuous, but also whether the person is useful, and has right ideas about public service.[6]

If congressmen, judges, legislators, mayors, or other public servants are not honestly or truly representing the people, if they are not carrying out the will of the people in their official actions, this simply proves that the people have not selected the right kind of men to represent them. There are honest men; there are men who are tried and loyal and patriotic. They are our neighbors. We have the choice of selecting them if we want to. *The truth is* that nearly all public officers are honest and patriotic. The truth is that as a rule they try to do what the people want. But *the truth is* that the majority of the American people take so little interest in public affairs that they make no effort to have their servants in public life know what they do want. People are ready to criticise if a mistake is made, but they will do little to help avoid mistakes.

I'll tell you what I would like to see. I'd like to see this assembly room in this school filled one night each week with children and men and women, with parents and teachers. It would be a real community meeting to talk over community, State, and National matters. I would like to see such a meeting in every school in this city, in this State, and in the Nation. I wish someone would start a movement to have the movies closed one evening each week, so that the people might have at least one night to give some little consideration to the serious problems of life. "Eternal vigilance is the price of liberty." Vigilance means watchfulness, care, and thought. Every man, woman, and child in America should watch and pray that our liberties so dearly bought with the life blood of heroes should not be taken away.

NOTES AND COMMENTS

1. **James Bryce** has written of our government: "The American Union is......a state which, while one, is nevertheless composed of other states even more essential to its existence than it is to theirs."

2. Constitution of the United States, Amendment XIV. Sec. I.

A person may attain to citizenship in the United States in any of seven different ways: 1. By birth—i. e. natural born. 2. By naturalization, which usually requires continuous residence for five years. 3. By treaty regulation. 4. By statute of Congress. 5. By annexation of territory. 6. By marriage—if a foreign woman marries an American citizen. 7. By honorable discharge from the army or navy, upon which the court admits to citizenship regardless of the time of residence in the United States.

In the United States we recognize a dual citizenship—citizenship in the United States, and citizenship in a State. Any person who is a citizen of the United States is also a citizen of the State wherein he or she resides. Nine different States grant the right of suffrage and State citizenship to such foreigners as take out their first naturalization papers. These States are Alabama, Arkansas, Indiana, Kansas, Missouri, Nebraska, Oregon, South Dakota, and Texas.

Citizenship must not be confused with the right of suffrage. Neither one necessarily includes the other. All citizens cannot vote—children for example. All voters are not necessarily citizens, those in the above nine States for example.

Aliens in the United States have practically all the civil rights that are enjoyed by citizens, but they do not have political rights. An alien may purchase, own, and convey property. He may sue and be sued in the courts.

"There can be no doubt that the minimum expectation of the framers of this amendment to the Constitution was that it would make the first eight amendments to the Constitution binding upon the states, as they already were upon the Federal Government, and that it should be susceptible not only of negative enforcement by the courts but also of direct positive enforcement by Congress."—*Cyclopedia of American Government*, Vol. II, p. 41.

3. Constitution of the United States, Amendment XV.

4. "By a series of decisions the most important of which were those in the Slaughter House cases (16 Wallace 36) and in the Civil Rights Cases (109 U. S. 3) the United States Supreme Court established the following principles: (1) that the prohibitions of the fourteenth amendment are addressed to the states as such and not to private individuals; (2) that these prohibitions contemplate only positive state acts and not acts of omission; (3) that the amendment recognizes a distinction between state citizenship and United States citizenship; (4) that it protects from state abridgement only 'the privileges and immunities' which the Constitution by its other provisions bestows upon 'citizens of the United States' as such."—*Cyclopedia of American Government*, Vol. II, p. 41.

The nineteenth amendment which is now ratified by the States, provides that "the right of citizens of the United States to vote shall not be denied or abridged by the United States or by any State on account of sex."—Constitution of the United States, Amendment XIX.

5. "The good citizen must in the first place, recognize what he owes his fellow citizens. If he is worthy to live in a free republic he must keep before his eyes his duty to the nation of which he forms a part. He

must keep himself informed, and he must think of himself as well as of the great questions of the day; and he must know how to express his thoughts."—Theodore Roosevelt.

6. In receiving applications for the many appointments which it was his duty to make, President Taylor said: "I shall make honesty, capacity and fidelity indispensable requisites to the bestowal of office; and the absence of any one of these qualities shall be deemed sufficient cause for removal."

ELEMENTARY QUESTIONS

1. Show how the United States gave citizens of the different States equal rights.
2. Who can vote in the United States? Who are citizens of the United States?
3. Is the power to vote simply a privilege?
4. Why is it that our representatives sometimes do not truly represent us?
5. How can we interest people in voting?

ADVANCED QUESTIONS

A. Show how it is important that people should have equal rights in the various States.
B. Give some illustrations of the variations from State to State of certain local laws, such as automobile laws, etc.
C. If the law of New York limits the speed of an automobile to 25 miles per hour and the law of Massachusetts limits the speed to 20 miles per hour, can a citizen of New York travelling in Massachusetts legally operate his car at 25 miles per hour? Under like circumstances can a citizen of Massachusetts while in New York operate his car at 25 miles per hour?
D. Show in detail the dangers of not voting.
E. How may a person obtain citizenship?
F. What has education to do with citizenship or voting?
G. Should you vote for a neighbor simply out of friendship? What should be taken into consideration?
H. Discuss Roosevelt's definition of a good citizen given in Note 5.
I. Outline a proper program for a community meeting.
J. Write a paper on the following:
   The Privileges of the Citizen
   The Danger of Not Voting
   The Ballot—An Obligation Not a Privilege
   How to Become a Naturalized Citizen
   Voting and other Duties of Citizenship

XIX

WRIT OF HABEAS CORPUS

THE PRIVILEGE OF THE WRIT OF HABEAS CORPUS NOT TO BE SUSPENDED EXCEPT IN WAR

Here is something in our Constitution which I suppose you have read, but which you probably do not understand. That is, you probably do not understand its real value, not to somebody else, but to yourselves, because all of these provisions of the Constitution are for each one of us.

We may go along through life, never being placed in a position where we will have to call upon the Constitution to defend us. Most of our people are peaceful and just, and it isn't often that the rights of innocent persons are attacked or invaded. It isn't often that an innocent man is arrested for a crime, and yet such a thing may occur any day to any one of us. You may rest assured that such things do not occur as often as they would if the Constitution did not stand as a barrier to protect innocent persons. These great constitutional guaranties are not only valuable when we want to assert our rights, but they are valuable as a restraint upon wrongdoers.[1]

Now here is this provision:

"The Privilege of the Writ of Habeas Corpus shall not be suspended, unless when in Cases of Rebellion or Invasion the public Safety may require it."[2]

What is a "writ of habeas corpus"? "Habeas Corpus" is a Latin phrase, which in English means "you may have the body". A writ of habeas corpus is a writ directed to the person detaining another, or holding him in prison, commanding him to produce the prisoner at a certain time and place before a court or judge, so that the right of imprisonment or

144

restraint may be inquired into. It is an ancient writ, recognized as far back in English jurisprudence as 1679. It was used against the king in the reign of Henry VII, and on through the later years. It was recognized from time to time, sometimes entirely denied, and again given force.

But as applied to you and to me, what does it signify? Suppose on your way home this evening, some person should seize you and force you to go to jail, and lock you up. No charge is made against you. You are innocent of any offense. You sit there in the cell wondering what it all means. You cannot even communicate with your parents or friends. The jail is built of stone, the iron bars are strong, and you are helpless.

Well, in the olden days, many a man and woman had such experiences, and many a man and many a woman lay in jail for long periods without any charge, or any trial, deprived of liberty, utterly powerless.

Now as I said, suppose you were in jail to-night—not even permitted to communicate with a friend or with a lawyer, and your father found out where you were. He could not go and break down the prison walls. He could not even talk to you; but if he were familiar with the Constitution of the United States and of his State—because there is a like provision in the Constitutions of all States—if your father understood his constitutional rights, he would at once apply to some court or judge for a writ of habeas corpus. It would be a simple matter. He would set out in writing the facts, simply the story that you were seized and were imprisoned wrongfully, and he would ask that a writ of habeas corpus issue, and this request, no court or judge can deny. He would promptly issue the writ, which would be in writing directed to the person keeping you in jail, or the keeper of the jail, or some one who was aiding in keeping you in jail, and this writ would command such person to have you brought before the court at once, "commanding him to produce the body of the prisoner at a certain time and place". You would be brought there, and the person having you in jail would have to show cause for such conduct. Unless legal cause were shown, the judge would promptly discharge you, and the person who had committed the wrong against you would probably receive proper punishment, after a trial, for his wrongful act.

Now there were long periods of time in England when the right to a writ of habeas corpus was suspended, during which time a person wrongfully in prison had no relief and no remedy, when helpless men and women starved and died. So when the Constitution was adopted, the people of America were careful to see that the following guaranty was written therein:

"The Privilege of the Writ of Habeas Corpus shall not be suspended".[3]

Under our Constitution this may be done only "in case of rebellion or invasion" when "public safety may require it". For instance, in the World War, which you all remember, some dangerous person, some traitor, might have been arrested by the military authorities and detained in custody, and he could not be discharged upon a writ of habeas corpus, because a state of war existed, and public safety required that he be held. Of course in times of war persons engaged in the military service are not entitled to a trial in a civil court for their offense. They are tried for military offenses by court martial. That is a military court, where the judges are military officers, ordered by their superiors to sit and hear the evidence. There is not much formality. In grave offenses prompt action is necessary. Spies are caught, the courts organized, the evidence taken, a finding of guilty made, and the party shot, all perhaps within twenty-four hours. These are the necessary awful consequences of war.

But can't you see now what a sense of security this little provision of our Constitution ought to bring to each one of us? We always know that in case of our wrongful arrest, a writ of habeas corpus will bring us before some court where we may have prompt inquiry into the reasons for invading our right to liberty, and prompt order for discharge if the arrest is not justified.

This writ issues not only in behalf of persons confined in jails and prisons, but also in every case where one is held by force against his will by another person, because this is a free country, and no man, whether a private citizen or public officer, has any power to restrain another against his will, unless such restraint is under legal proceedings with all the safeguards of the Constitution.

I remember a case when unfortunately a father and mother were separated and divorced. Their little boy was left with his mother. The judge decided that the father was a bad man and that he was not worthy to have charge of his son.

A few months later that father went to the house where the mother and boy lived, watched behind the hedge until the little boy was at play in the yard, when he seized him, jumped in an automobile which was waiting for him in the woods, and drove away at great speed. He took the boy to a boarding school in a neighboring State, telling the principal of the school that he wanted the boy safely kept until he should return from Europe. After many days the sheriff with the aid of detectives found where the boy was. The mother came to the school. Of course she was filled with joy when she saw her son. She thought that she could take him away with her at once, but the principal would not consent. He said that he had no knowledge of whether or not she was the boy's mother; that she had no right to take him away; and that his duty was to return the boy to the man who had left him in the school. The appeal of the mother and the tears of the boy were in vain.

At last she had to leave the boy. She at once consulted a lawyer. He prepared a written application asking that a writ of habeas corpus be issued, commanding the principal of the school to bring the boy before the judge, that the judge might hear the evidence, and make an order releasing the boy from the school and placing him in the charge of his mother. The writ was issued by the judge. An officer went to the school, read the writ to the principal, who promptly brought the boy to the court room.

There the judge heard the story of the mother and the simple tale of the little boy, he examined certified copies of the order of the court awarding the custody of the boy to his mother, which the sheriff had procured, and then he very promptly ordered the principal of the school to give the boy to his mother. The principal was of course glad to do so, when he found that the father had done wrong.

This is only one of hundreds of cases where the writ of habeas corpus releases someone from wrongful confinement. Such wrongful confinement may be in a school or in a home or in a jail or in a dungeon or in a dark cellar. No matter where, the writ of habeas corpus does not stop at locked doors or barred windows or stone walls. An officer with such a writ can break and enter if necessary. No obstacle can be allowed wrongfully to deprive an American citizen of his liberty.

NOTES AND COMMENTS

1. "The American Constitution is the most wonderful work ever struck off at a given moment by the brain and purpose of man."—William E. Gladstone.

"It will be the wonder and admiration of all future generations and the model of all future constitutions."—William Pitt.

"Our fathers by an almost divine prescience, struck the golden mean," when they made the Constitution.—Pomeroy.

"It (The U. S. Constitution) ranks above every other written constitution for the intrinsic excellence of its scheme, its adaptation to the circumstances of the people, the simplicity, brevity and precision of its language, its judicious mixture of definition in principle with elasticity in details."—James Bryce.

2. "This is the most famous writ in the law; and, having for many centuries been employed to remove illegal restraint upon personal liberty, no matter by what power imposed, it is often called the great writ of liberty."—Bouvier's *Law Dictionary*, Vol. I, p. 917.

3. In 1861 Chief Justice Taney decided in the United States Circuit Court of Maryland that Congress alone possessed the power under the Constitution to suspend the writ.—9 *American Law Register*, 524.

The privilege of the writ is, however, necessarily suspended whenever martial law is declared in force; for martial law suspends all civil process.

"As a recognized legal remedy, resort to the proceeding by habeas corpus may be had where a person is imprisoned under pretended legal authority which in fact for any reason is absolutely void, as where the warrant of arrest or commitment is insufficient or the proceeding under which the warrant was issued was without legal authority."

"A state court or judge cannot inquire by habeas corpus into the validity of arrest or detention of a person under federal authority. The right to redress in such cases, if any, must be sought in the Federal courts. But on the other hand Federal courts and judges may inquire into the cause of the restraint of liberty of any person by a state when the justification of Federal authority or immunity is set up for the act complained of."—*Cyclopedia of American Government*, Vol. II, p. 106.

ELEMENTARY QUESTIONS

1. What is a writ of habeas corpus?
2. What does "habeas corpus" mean?
3. When was it recognized in England?
4. When may it be suspended in America?
5. Just what does it mean to the average citizen?
6. Can you think of a time when it might be valuable to you?
7. What is martial law?

ADVANCED QUESTIONS

A. Just when is a writ of habeas corpus likely to prove valuable?
B. Why is it called "the most famous writ of the law"?
C. Show how it affects the poor man.
D. Show how it makes for democracy.
E. Write a paper on the following:
Abuses Found Before the Writ of Habeas Corpus Was Recognized
Cases Where It was Used Locally
The Experience of the Arrest of an Innocent Man Who Was Unable to Furnish Bail
A Court Martial

XX

OTHER PROHIBITED LAWS

NO BILL OF ATTAINDER OR EX POST FACTO LAW MAY BE PASSED BY CONGRESS

This morning I have something else for you which you probably do not understand, something that you can hardly imagine would interest you personally; but as I have often repeated, always bear in mind that every single clause of the Constitution is made for each and every one of us, no matter what position we may have in life.

The framers of the Constitution said:

"No Bill of Attainder or ex post facto Law shall be passed."[1]

What does "attainder" mean? It means the extinction of civil rights and capacities and powers, which under the law in the olden times took place whenever a person was convicted of treason, or of a crime for which the death sentence was imposed. It means that all the estate of the convicted person, all his land, money, or other property, was forfeited to the government; so that upon his death nothing passed by inheritance to his heirs. As it was expressed, his blood was "corrupted". He could not sue in a court of justice. He was helpless to defend any right of himself or his family.

By "bills of attainder", which were legislative acts imposing that penalty on the accused without giving him any hearing in a court, many persons were deprived of their rights and their possessions in the centuries which have gone by, in order that such rights and such possessions might go to some favorite of the government. Of course no one would have much sympathy for a person who might be actually guilty of treason, or guilty of a great crime which involved a death penalty; but in the olden days innocent men were often charged with treason and punished. Conspiracies were formed to get rid of certain individuals who might be an obstacle to the achievement of base ambitions.

The abuses arising out of the imposition of attainder became so grave that in the time of Queen Victoria a statute was passed in England abolishing the extreme penalties which followed it.

In some of the colonies in this country, before the Constitution was adopted, acts of attainder were passed and enforced; but when the Constitution was finally adopted, bills of attainder were forever barred.

Don't you see the spirit of charity which is manifest in this, just as in the entire Constitution, charity even for wrongdoers, charity for the weaknesses of men? Wrongdoers of course must be punished, yet the Constitution wipes out harsh and brutal methods which were common in the days before America came into being.

No "ex post facto law" shall be passed. *What does that mean?*[2] If a person does an act, which at the time of the doing of the act is not a criminal offense, the Congress of the United States, with all its power, cannot make that act, innocent when done, a crime. Yet this used to be done in the old days. You can imagine how in those days a brutal government being desirous of getting rid of some objectionable person, but desiring to have its acts appear legal, might find that he had done some act which was not punishable under the law; but through a corrupt legislative body, it might so legislate as to make the act a criminal offense, and thus have the person tried and convicted.

A person might commit an offense for which there was a moderate punishment; and the legislature might, after the commission of the crime, but before he was tried, increase the penalty. For instance, if there were a penalty of two years imprisonment for stealing a horse, and some neighbor was guilty of stealing a horse, thus leaving himself, when convicted, subject to two years imprisonment, all the powers of the United States government, all the powers of Congress, all the wonderful power of the people of the country could not change the penalty, could not, for instance, amend the law so as to provide a five year penalty instead of two, so as to affect this neighbor who had stolen the horse before this time. He could, if convicted, be sentenced to two years, but no more.

You may think that those who adopted the Constitution must have been suspicious of Congress, or the people in thus carefully preventing wrongs against individuals accused of a crime—yes, individuals who had actually committed a crime; but you can readily understand why they were so careful. The conduct of the governments of the world had been such before that day that suspicion was justified. The Constitution was made for the individual—for men, women, and children—to guard their rights against the abuse of power; and in fact most of the wrongs of the world have had their origin in the abuse of power. The Constitution guards the humblest person against abuse of the power granted to the government, as well as against the wrongs of our neighbors.

The people in this country have great power—absolute power. This power may be expressed in laws enacted by Congress or by the legislatures of the States, except in those things which the people themselves in the Constitution of the United States, and in the Constitutions of the different States, have placed beyond even their own power.

Of course these provisions of the Constitution, as all provisions of the Constitution, may be changed by the people, but not by a mere majority of the people. These constitutional provisions relate to sacred rights, and they may not be changed except upon mature deliberation, and by a vote which represents the sentiment of at least a majority of the people of three-fourths of the States.

So I hope you can realize that when the framers of the Constitution prohibited bills of attainder, and prohibited the enactment of the ex post facto laws, they were doing something for the people of this country. They had the rights of the people in mind—the rights of the humble and perhaps unknown, as well as the rights of those in high places. I do not expect you to study the details of these provisions of the Constitution relating to bills of attainder and ex post facto laws. You will probably never have to enforce these rights which are given to you under the Constitution. I hope you will not; but the important thing which I always want you to bear in mind is, that these guaranties of the Constitution are in existence and that they confer upon you certain powers which may be asserted to protect your liberty if occasion should ever arise.

I am sure you realize that at the beginning of the life of the American Nation, extreme care was exercised by those who framed the Constitution, to guard the people at every point against injustice and wrong, whether exercised by private individuals or by public officials.

Understanding these things—feeling these things, will give you a new sense of power, of pride, and of duty, as citizens of this great Nation.

NOTES AND COMMENTS

1. Constitution of the United States, Art. I, Sec. 9, Cl. 3.
"The effect of attainder upon a felon is, in general terms, that all his estate, real and personal, is forfeited; that his blood is corrupted, and so nothing passes by inheritance to, from or through him."

"In the United States the doctrine of attainder is now scarcely known, although during and shortly after the Revolution acts of attainder were passed by several of the states. The passage of such bills is expressly forbidden by the Constitution."—Bouvier's *Law Dictionary*, Vol. I, p. 190.

"A bill of attainder, as thought of in the United States to-day, would be such law as permitted a person charged with the commission of a crime, to be tried and found guilty and sentenced without being present at the trial." It is one of the rules of procedure in court to-day that in all criminal cases the person charged with crime must be present during the entire trial. Another fundamental judicial fact is that all criminal punishment terminates with the death of the person found guilty; his children are exempt.

2. "An ex-post-facto law is a law which in its operation makes an act criminal which was not criminal at the time the act was committed, or provides a more severe punishment for criminal acts already committed, or changes the rules of procedure so as to make it more difficult for one accused of crime to defend in a prosecution of such crime." "The prohibition relates to retroactive criminal statutes providing a punishment for an act previously committed or increasing the punishment making it more difficult for the accused to defend, but not to retroactive laws, even though criminal, which mitigate the punishment or merely change or regulate the procedure without imposing any additional substantial burden on the accused in making his defense."—*Cyclopedia of American Government*, Vol. I, p. 700.

We should keep in mind that both "bills of attainder" and "ex post facto" laws have only to do with crimes and their punishment. These laws do not relate to civil matters.

ELEMENTARY QUESTIONS

1. What does attainder mean?
2. What was the effect of a bill of attainder on the family of a man who was convicted?
3. Why does the abolition of attainder show the charity of the founders of the Constitution?
4. What is an ex post facto law?
5. How would this kind of a law be unjust?
6. How could a strong, powerful, and dishonest man work injustice by means of such a law?

ADVANCED QUESTIONS

A. Show how attainder worked in England in the early days.
B. What were the abuses found under such a law?
C. Show how its abolition made for democracy.
D. Show how the abolition of ex post facto laws made for democracy.
E. Write a paper on the following:
   The Injustice of Attainder
   The Injustice of an Ex Post Facto Law

XXI

TITLES, GIFTS, TREASON

PROHIBITION OF TITLES AND FOREIGN GIFTS—TREASON,
ITS TRIAL AND PUNISHMENT

America is a democracy. It was the plan from the beginning that it always should be a democracy. The human race had suffered much from royalty, from kings and emperors, and queens and princes. Human nature is weak. We are all more or less attracted by people with titles. Story books which we read in childhood exalt the "lords" and "ladies" and "princes", and I regret to say that the history of lords and ladies and princes does not always justify the pictures which our story books would paint for us.

The men who framed the Constitution had just finished a life and death struggle with royalty—a struggle between the people and a king, and the people had won. They were determined that the blighting influence of royal power should never again find a place on American soil. Therefore they put into the Constitution:

"No Title of Nobility shall be granted by the United States: And no Person holding any Office of Profit or Trust under them, shall, without the Consent of the Congress, accept of any present, Emolument, Office, or Title, of any kind whatever, from any King, Prince, or foreign State."[1]

Never before in the history of the world was such a bold thing done. These words reflect the spirit of the Revolution. They mark the turning point in the history of human governments. They proclaim the final establishment of the government by the people—the first real government by the people that the world ever knew.

I wonder if those who criticise the government of America who complain that in this country the people have no chance, ever read these glowing words of our Constitution. It isn't so much the words, but the spirit in which they were made a part of our Constitution, the spirit in which the young Nation proclaimed to the world eternal separation from kingly power.

I find all through the Constitution an expression of grim determination to fortify the Nation against any influence which would weaken the supreme power of the people, which would in any way interfere with the plan to make this a government by the people.

In many provisions of our Constitution we find expressions which show how humane America is.

We hate treason. In fact there is no crime so dark, so awful, as treason. But in the history of the world, treason has meant many things, and unfortunately treason has been made not only the instrument of those who sought the destruction of the governments, but it has sometimes been made the instrument of tyrants in suppressing the rights, and in crushing the hopes of the people. It all depends on what is meant by treason.

In the olden days we find men charged with treason when the offense was in fact very slight—perhaps a just resistance to the king, perhaps merely an assertion of natural human right against the king.

The government of the United States being intended to protect the liberties of the people, the Constitution put a bar against prosecution for treason, except where the accused was actually an enemy of his country, endeavoring to aid in the destruction of his country. We are here told what treason is:

"Treason against the United States, shall consist only in

levying War against them, or in adhering to their Enemies, giving them Aid and Comfort. No person shall be convicted of Treason unless on the Testimony of two Witnesses to the same overt Act, or on Confession in open Court.

"The Congress shall have power to declare the Punishment of Treason, but no Attainder of Treason shall work Corruption of Blood, or Forfeiture except during the Life of the Person Attainted."[2]

We see all through the Constitution a splendid spirit of justice, and a spirit of charity, even toward the guilty. By this article of the Constitution, not only is treason defined, but any conviction of a person for treason must be upon the testimony of at least two witnesses to the same act, or upon a confession in open court.

The innocent must not be punished; and the guilty, when convicted, shall alone bear the punishment. Treason being such a grave offense, Congress may, if it so desires, provide very severe penalties, but it cannot attaint the blood, so that the children or the grandchildren of the guilty person shall suffer as in the olden days; nor shall the right of forfeiture of property obtain, except during the life of the person guilty of treason.

No one objects to any penalty, however severe, where treason is proved, but it is contrary to the spirit of America to brand the innocent descendants of one who is guilty of a crime. Of course the children of the guilty will always bear a certain degree of reproach from their fellowmen, but it is not fair that they should be visited with penalties for an offense which they themselves never committed. It is the spirit of America that each person shall enjoy any position in life which he may win by merit and honest endeavor, and no obstacle should be placed in his way by the wrong of an unfortunate ancestor.

NOTES AND COMMENTS

1. Constitution of the United States, Art. 1, Sec. 8.

Titles of nobility as recognized in many European countries include the following: duke, earl, marquis, viscount, and baron. These titles were in part hereditary and in part acquired. They always conferred special privileges both in rank and in political preferment. Such titles cannot exist in a democracy because they in their very nature destroy equality before the law, and that is the fundamental principle of democratic government.

"The provisions prohibiting the granting of titles of nobility are designed, no doubt, first to preserve equality before the law, and second, to secure in perpetuity a republican form of government. Such provisions are not essential to theoretical equality before the law, for such equality is fundamental in the law of England notwithstanding the existence of titles of nobility. But the framers of the Constitution evidently contemplated a form of government in which there should be no special privileges conferred by rank or title. The additional provision in the Federal Constitution prohibiting the acceptance by any person holding any office of profit or trust under the United States of any present, emolument, office or title from any foreign sovereign or power without the consent of Congress, was probably intended to prevent the exercise of foreign influence in governmental affairs. These articles in the Constitution are substantially borrowed from the Articles of Confederation."—Emlin McClain, quoted in the *Cyclopedia of American Government*, Vol. II, p. 58.

2. Constitution of the United States, Art. III, Sec. 3, Cl. 1.

Treason is defined in this article of the Constitution and therefore Congress cannot define it in any other manner. Many people use the word "treason" very loosely. They often speak of a person committing treason when the act committed is not treasonable at all, but is some less severe crime. Treason consists only in levying war against the United States or in giving aid or comfort to enemies of the United States.

The meaning of "two witnesses to the same **overt** act" is that the Constitution requires that two persons will appear in court and swear to the fact that they personally saw the act committed. "Overt act" means "openly committed act". Chief Justice John Marshall knew that in the trial of Aaron Burr it would be impossible to get two persons to swear to having seen Burr commit the conspiracy, so he took advantage of the technicality in the indictment and threw the case out of court. This trial was held at Richmond, Virginia.

"Confession in open court" is about the only instance in which such confession will convict a person charged with committing a crime. As a rule a person's own confession will not be accepted as evidence against him, in criminal prosecutions, because few confessions are made without some threat or inducement and under the guaranty (p. 99) that a person cannot be compelled to be a witness against himself they are excluded.

ELEMENTARY QUESTIONS

1. America is a democracy. Why does this mean so much?
2. What does that phrase bring to mind?
3. Why did we abolish all titles of nobility?
4. What is treason?
5. Why is it limited so carefully?

ADVANCED QUESTIONS

A. What was the real purpose of abolishing all titles of nobility?

B. Why did the founders of the Constitution refuse to permit our representatives to accept gifts from abroad?

C. What acts are treason to-day?

D. Show how these provisions make for democracy?

E. Write a paper on the following:

An Illustration of an Act of Treason During the World War

How A Person May Obtain a Responsible Position in Life

Laws Which Retard Advancement in Life

XXII

JURY, EXCEPT IN IMPEACHMENT

CRIMINAL TRIALS, EXCEPT IMPEACHMENT, TO BE BY JURY —EQUAL RIGHTS—NO RELIGIOUS TEST FOR OFFICE

There are still three articles of the Constitution containing personal guaranties but the substance of these articles has been considered in connection with other articles already discussed. They are the following:

"The trial of all Crimes, except in Cases of Impeachment, shall be by Jury, and such Trial shall be held in the State where the said crimes shall have been committed; but when not committed within any State, the Trial shall be at such Place or Places as the Congress may by Law have directed."[1]

"The Citizens of each State shall be entitled to all Privileges and Immunities of Citizens in the several States."[2]

"No religious Test shall ever be required as a Qualification to any Office or public Trust under the United States."[3]

Here again we see emphasized the right of trial by jury. I want you to give some thought to this particular right, because it applies not only to cases where persons are accused of a crime, but also to nearly all cases involving property rights.

The ordinary lawsuit, where one person is suing another to recover money, property, or damages, is triable by a jury. You understand of course the purpose of a trial. As already explained the main thing in every trial is to determine the truth as to the points in dispute, and the truth in such cases under our Constitution is determined, not by judges, but by jurors, men from the ordinary walks of life, your neighbors, men accustomed to dealing with ordinary human affairs. This right is important in aiding a person to have the truth properly established; but it is especially important, as I have heretofore explained, because it emphasizes the fact that this is a government by the people, and that in grave emergencies when life, liberty, or property, is in danger, the representatives of the common people, selected from the ranks of the common people, shall be the judges.

Of course I have fully explained to you, and I do not wish to have any confusion upon that point, that the judges themselves are also representatives of the people, because they are elected by the people, or appointed by those agents of the people who are elected by the people.

I have intentionally repeated, sometimes over and over, rules and reasons, because we must have them in our minds so that they will never be forgotten.

Now as above explained, the citizens of each State are guaranteed the right to go to another State, and exercise in that other State the same rights as the citizens of that State. This is in the spirit of America which gives us all equal opportunity. A citizen of Massachusetts going to the State of Minnesota has the same rights in Minnesota as the citizens of Minnesota have. Minnesota could not discriminate against him because he was a citizen of another State. Of course he could not exercise rights which the citizens of Minnesota were not entitled to, but all rights of the citizens of Minnesota are guaranteed to him while he is in that State.

Now as to the provision which forever bars any religious test as the qualification for any office or place of public trust under the United States. We have already given serious consideration to the great fundamental human privilege which the Constitution guards, the right to worship God according to the dictates of one's conscience. We have already found that regardless of church or creed each person stands before the law equal in our country. The older you grow, the more fully you realize what religion means to a great many people in this world, the more fully you will appreciate the blessing which came to humanity in these provisions of the Constitution. There are some of us who do not belong to any church organization, and yet we are intensely interested, because there was a time when every person was compelled by law to belong to a church organization, to the state church, the state religion. I have already explained that we find solemn statutes enacted by the British Parliament, as an illustration, which provided for a death penalty for those who did not believe in the religion of the state.

There is no religious test which can be made a qualification for any office under the United States; nor for any office for any State in the Union. There should be no individual discrimination in voting for public officials because of the religion or church to which a candidate for office may belong. These are sacred, individual rights. Men must be judged by their conduct, by their character, by their ability, by their capacity to serve the people and their country, not by the religion which one may profess.

We must cultivate the spirit of charity toward our neighbors, charity which means love, which enables us to maintain a proper spirit of toleration for those who differ from us in matters of belief.

NOTES AND COMMENTS

1. Constitution of the United States, Art. III, Sec. 2, Cl. 3.
Impeachment is the manner of trial fixed by the Constitution for the trial and removal of Federal officers who are accused of treason, bribery, and other high crimes and misdemeanors. Congress alone has the power of conducting an impeachment of Federal officers. The legislature of a State has the power of impeaching State officers. Impeachment, as the word is commonly used, includes both accusation and trial. The "impeachment" or accusation is brought by a two-thirds vote of the lower house, and the trial and conviction or acquittal is carried on by the upper house. Andrew Johnson, President of the United States, was impeached—i. e. he was formally accused, but he was acquitted in his trial in the Senate. Conviction in an impeachment proceeding causes an officer to be removed from office and disqualified from ever holding any office of honor or trust under the government again. A person may be convicted and not given the full penalty. He may be only removed from office, but not disqualified from again holding office.

It is possible that a crime may be committed on a river that forms State boundaries. Where a river forms a boundary the middle of the main channel is made the boundary line. It is often difficult to determine on which side of the line the crime was committed, and both States may then claim to have jurisdiction over the case. This must be decided as any other fact in the case.

The manner of the trial in use, before jury trial was established, was by ordeal or by battle. In trial either by ordeal or by battle the issue was left to God to decide and He was thought to perform a miracle to reveal the guilt or innocence of the accused person. One form of ordeal was to compel the accused to plunge his arm into boiling water and if innocent the Lord would protect him from being scalded. Another form of ordeal was to compel the accused to walk barefoot over hot plow shares. If innocent the Lord would again protect his feet from being burned.

The first form of jury to displace the old ordeal or battle as a means of deciding guilt or innocence was the "compurgators" or "oath bearers". They comprised a group of men who would appear before the court and give oath that the accused was not a bad man and had committed no crime. They did not investigate the accusation, they only testified to the good character of the accused. If a man accused could not produce compurgators, he must undergo the ordeal. The duty of these oath bearers gradually became more extended until they became investigators, and finally became a grand jury.

2. Constitution of the United States, Art. IV, Sec. 2, Cl. 1.

"The right of a citizen of one state to pass through, or to reside in, any other state, for purposes of trade, agriculture, professional pursuits, or otherwise; to claim the benefit of habeas corpus; to institute and maintain actions of any kind in the courts of the state; to take, hold and dispose of property, either real or personal; and an exemption from higher taxes or impositions than are paid by the other citizens of the state; may be mentioned as some of the particular privileges and immunities of citizens, which are clearly embraced by the description."—Corfield vs. Coryell, *Washington C. C. Rep.* 380.

3. Constitution of the United States, Art. 6, Cl. 3.

While no religious test of any kind may ever be required from any officer of the United States as a condition of his being elected, or holding office, public sentiment nevertheless favors Christian character among the people. If a candidate for office were an atheist and made public confession as to his lack of belief in God, it would doubtless mitigate against his election.

"The general principle of equality of all persons before the law excludes discriminations made on account of religious belief, with the result that religious tests should not be made the basis of political rights or for determining qualifications for office or in general for the possession, exercise, or protection of civil rights."—Emlin McClain, quoted in the *Cyclopedia of American Government*, Vol. III, p. 176.

"This clause was introduced for the double purpose of satisfying the scruples of many persons who feel an invincible repugnance to any religious test or affirmation, and to cut off forever every pretence of any alliance between church and state in the national government."—Story's Const. Sc. 1841.

ELEMENTARY QUESTIONS

1. Does a citizen have the same rights in California that he does in New York?
2. Why is religious belief never made a qualification for office?
3. What is impeachment?
4. Are judges representatives of the people? Why?
5. Can the State of Nebraska enact a law imposing a tax upon merchandise shipped into Nebraska from any other State?

ADVANCED QUESTIONS

A. What is impeachment?
B. Describe the manner of trial before trial by jury. Compare the justice of the ordeal and wager of battle with the jury system.
C. Show how these provisions make for democracy.
D. Why is the spirit of charity necessary in a democracy?
E. Write a paper on the following:
    The Ordeal
    Wager of Battle
    How Englishmen Won the Right to Trial by Jury

XXIII

WRONGS UNDER KING GEORGE

THE STORY OF THE COLONISTS IN THE DECLARATION OF INDEPENDENCE

When we first read over the numerous guaranties of the Constitution protecting the American people in their rights, we sometimes wonder why certain provisions were inserted in the Constitution. Being born here in America, never having been compelled to submit to the abuse of arbitrary power, and always having lived under the Constitution, and always being guarded by its provisions against the abuse of power, we can hardly understand why it was necessary to make so many provisions against things which we can hardly imagine ever happened in human government.

Whenever you have a chance, read somethings of the governments of the world under kings or other absolute rulers. In fact, we cannot understand the blessings of our government until we know something of what our ancestors were compelled to submit to under the governments of the different countries of the world a few centuries ago.

While we have in mind the guaranties of our Constitution, it is well for us to have clearly in mind some of the definite things which the framers of the Constitution had before them, some of the wrongs which the human race had endured at the hands of government which the framers of the Constitution were determined the people of America would never have to endure. You can hardly imagine what little regard or consideration was given to human rights in those old days now almost forgotten. I am not going to undertake to discuss the problems of government in different countries of the world.[1] The purpose which I have in mind can be fully served by a consideration of the government in this country under the king of Great Britain during the years preceding the Revolutionary War. You understand, of course, that even at that time a great advance had been made in recognizing certain rights of the people. In fact, I think it is generally recognized that England before the American Revolution had attained nearer to a fairly just government than any other country in the world up to that time. There had been many periods during its history when the people had asserted themselves and had forced the recognition of certain rights by the government—by the king, and yet it was still a government by a king. It was a government under a king to which the colonies owed allegiance. It was government under a king against which the colonies finally revolted. It was government under a king which brought about the Revolution. It was resistance to government under a king which inspired the heroes who won the liberty of the new world. It was the brutality of a government under a king which inspired the framers of the Constitution so carefully to guard against the abuses which the world had known before liberty had been established on American soil. I will not undertake to recite for you the things which the people were compelled to endure under this government of a king. I will let the people of the colonies tell their story. You remember that in 1776, after the beginning of the Revolutionary War, the people of the Colonies adopted the Declaration of Independence which recites in detail the abuses and wrongs they had endured under a government by a king. It is one of the most dramatic recitals in history. Let these colonies tell their own story. I am not going to read the entire Declaration of Independence; I am simply going to read the recital therein of the wrongs which came to the people, the men, women, and children, the human beings, who up to that time were compelled to live here in America under the government of a king.

The history of the present king of Great Britain is a history of repeated injuries and usurpations, all having in direct object the establishment of an absolute tyranny over these states. To prove this, let facts be submitted to a candid world.

He has refused his assent to laws the most wholesome and necessary for the public good.

He has forbidden his governors to pass laws of immediate and pressing importance, unless suspended in their operation till his assent should be obtained, and, when so suspended, he has utterly neglected to attend to them.

He has refused to pass other laws for the accommodation of large districts of people, unless those people would relinquish the right of representation in the legislature—a right inestimable to them, and formidable to tyrants only.

He has called together legislative bodies at places unusual, uncomfortable, and distant from the repository of their public records for the sole purpose of fatiguing them into compliance with his measures.

He has dissolved representative houses repeatedly for opposing, with manly firmness, his invasions on the rights of the people.

He has refused, for a long time after such dissolutions, to cause others to be elected; whereby the legislative powers, incapable of annihilation, have returned to the people at large for their exercise; the state remaining, in the mean time, exposed to all dangers of invasion from without, and convulsions within.

He has endeavored to prevent the population of these states; for that purpose obstructing the laws of naturalization of foreigners; refusing to pass others to encourage their migration hither and raising the conditions of new appropriations of lands.

He has obstructed the administration of justice by refusing his assent to laws for establishing judiciary powers.

He has made judges dependent on his will alone for the tenure of their offices and the amount and payment of their salaries.

He has erected a multitude of new offices, and sent hither swarms of officers to harass our people and eat out their substance.

He has kept among us, in times of peace, standing armies, without the consent of our legislatures.

He has affected to render the military independent of, and superior to, the civil power.

He has combined with others to subject us to a jurisdiction foreign to our constitution and unacknowledged by our laws, giving his assent to their acts of pretended legislation—

For quartering large bodies of armed troops among us;

For protecting them, by a mock trial, from punishment for any murders which they should commit on the inhabitants of these states;

For cutting off our trade with all parts of the world;

For imposing taxes upon us without our consent;

For depriving us, in many cases, of the benefits of trial by jury;

For transporting us beyond seas, to be tried for pretended offenses;

For abolishing the free system of English laws in a neighboring province; establishing therein an arbitrary government, and enlarging its boundaries, so as to render it at once an example and fit instrument for introducing the same absolute rule into these colonies;

For taking away our charters, abolishing our most valuable laws, and altering fundamentally the forms of our government;

For suspending our own legislatures, and declaring themselves invested with power to legislate for us in all cases whatsoever.

He has abdicated government here by declaring us out of his protection and waging war against us.

He has plundered our seas, ravaged our coasts, burnt our towns, and destroyed the lives of our people.

He is, at this time, transporting large armies of foreign mercenaries to complete the works of death, desolation and tyranny, already begun, with circumstances of cruelty and perfidy scarcely paralleled in the most barbarous ages, and totally unworthy the head of a civilized nation.

He has constrained our fellow-citizens, taken captive on the high seas, to bear arms against their country, to become the executioners of their friends and brethren, or to fall themselves by their hands.

He has excited domestic insurrections amongst us, and has endeavored to bring on the inhabitants of our frontiers the merciless Indian savages, whose known rule of warfare is an undistinguished destruction of all ages, sexes and conditions.

In every stage of these oppressions we have petitioned for redress, in the most humble terms; our repeated petitions have been answered only by repeated injury. A prince whose character is thus marked by every act which may define a tyrant is unfit to be the ruler of a free people.''

Now, if there be those who are not satisfied under the present government of America, let them reflect. Let them compare their rights to-day with the rights of the people subjected to the repeated "injuries and usurpations" so eloquently recited by those who founded this government, who adopted our Constitution which will forever bar any power from exercising "a design to reduce them (the people) to absolute despotism".

Read through this catalog of wrongs endured by the people of the colonies. Then read through the guaranties of the Constitution. You will find that in large part the guaranties of the Constitution were inspired by the wrongs recited by the people when they proclaimed their independence.[2]

I said that this recital is dramatic. It is also pathetic. Listen: *"In every stage of these oppressions we have petitioned for redress in the most humble terms; our repeated petitions have been answered only by repeated injury"*. Is it any wonder that the Constitution of the United States should provide that "Congress shall make no law . . . . abridging . . . . the right . . . . to petition the Government for a redress of grievances"?

Is it any wonder that we find in the Constitution guaranties of freedom of worship, freedom of speech and of the press, the right of the people to bear arms, the right of the people to be secure in their persons, houses, and papers, the right to a speedy jury trial when accused of crime, and the right to a trial in the district where the offense was committed instead of being sent beyond the seas? When we read of the wrongs endured by the people under the government by a king we can readily understand why the people put into their Constitution a guaranty that a person no matter how poor shall have an attorney to defend him, shall have his witnesses brought into court at government expense, that excessive bail shall not be required, and cruel and unusual punishments shall not be inflicted, that slavery is forever abolished on American soil, that the property of every person, rich or poor is sacred, and that even the government of the United States cannot take it for public use without just compensation, that every person shall have equal protection of the law, and if wrongfully imprisoned he can secure his release by writ of habeas corpus. You can readily see that all these guaranties of the Constitution and many others which we have been studying were intended to give protection to the people from wrongs which the people had suffered throughout the world under the different forms of government existing before America was born.

From the stirring story related by the people in the Declaration of Independence of the injustice which they had to suffer under a king, you can see how carefully future generations of people upon American soil were guarded by the Constitution against the wrongs which our forefathers had endured.

NOTES AND COMMENTS

1. A glance at the motives of Europeans in coming to America will reveal the fact that thousands of the best people of European countries left their homes to escape either religious or political persecution at the hands of the government or the king. Such was true of the Huguenots of France, the Pilgrims and Puritans of England, and only recently, the Jews of Russia.

The laws of "attainder" in England in the early times confiscated the property of persons, however innocent they themselves might be, if they were near relatives of other persons who had committed grave crimes.

Before the passage of the Habeas Corpus Act of 1679 in England, any person of royalty or high official standing in the government could falsely accuse another person of crime and cause that innocent person to languish in prison for years, or even for life, because he could not get before a court of justice to establish his innocence.

In many European countries the peasants were burdened wth taxes to support kings and courts without the slightest representation in the tax levying authority. In France, just preceding the French Revolution, the peasants were obliged to purchase a certain number of barrels of salt each year, without having the slightest use for the salt, because the crown lands produced salt and the revenues went to the king.

In many European countries a state church was established and the people obliged to support it by taxes levied against their property, regardless of whether it represented their religious beliefs.

2. A comparison of the provisions of the Declaration of Independence with those of the Constitution will show the wrongs of the English king righted by the Constitution.

Declaration of Independence—"He has refused assent to laws the most wholesome and necessary for the public good."

Constitution of the United States.—A bill if vetoed by the President may be repassed by two-thirds of the senate and house of representatives.

Declaration of Independence.—"He has forbidden his governors to pass laws of immediate and pressing importance."

Constitution of the United States.—Congress shall have the power to lay and collect taxes, duties, etc. (See Const. Art. I, S. 8.)

Declaration of Independence.—"He has dissolved representative houses repeatedly, for opposing with manly firmness, his invasions on the rights of the people."

Constitution of the United States.—Congress shall meet at the seat of government—once each year.

Declaration of Independence.—"He has refused, for a long time after dissolution, to cause others to be elected."

Constitution of the United States.—The time, place and manner of holding elections for Senators and Representatives, shall be prescribed in each State by the legislature thereof.

Declaration of Independence.—"He has obstructed the administration of justice."

Constitution of the United States.—Jurisdiction of Courts fixed by Constitution. Judges not responsible to the President, but to Congress, which represents the people.

Declaration of Independence.—"He has made judges dependent on his will alone."

Constitution of United States.—Judges subject to removal only by impeachment by Congress.

Declaration of Independence.—"He has kept standing armies . . . . without consent of the legislature."

Constitution of the United States.—"Congress shall have power to raise and support armies." "To provide and maintain a navy."

Declaration of Independence.—"For transporting us beyond seas to be tried for pretended offenses."

Constitution of the United States.—"Such trial shall be held in the state where said crime shall have been committed."

Declaration of Independence.—"For depriving us, in many cases, of the right of trial by jury."

Constitution of the United States.—"The trial of all crimes, except in case of impeachment, shall be by jury."

Declaration of Independence.—"For quartering large bodies of armed troops among us."

Constitution of the United States.—"No soldier shall in time of peace, be quartered in any house without the consent of the owner."

Declaration of Independence.—"For imposing taxes on us without our consent."

Constitution of the United States.—"Congress shall have power to levy and collect taxes."

ELEMENTARY QUESTIONS

1. When was the Declaration of Independence signed?
2. How long did the colonists of America continue under government by a king?
3. How did it happen to be drawn up?
4. Compare each sentence of this quotation (pages 167, 168) with the guaranties that you have discussed in class.

ADVANCED QUESTIONS

A. Discuss in detail the reasons for the coming of the American colonists.
B. Discuss in detail the contrasts noted in Note 2. Review the previous study with reference to our Declaration of Independence.
C. Write a paper comparing the solution found in the Constitution with the grievances noted in the Declaration.
D. Discuss a method by which this might be brought to the attention of the Socialists, Anarchists, and Bolsheviki who are criticising our government to-day.

XXIV

SHALL ANY PART BE REPEALED

WHAT PROVISIONS WOULD YOU HAVE TAKEN OUT OF THE CONSTITUTION

We have discussed the main personal guaranties of the Constitution. There is a large part of the Constitution which we have not yet considered. Not because I do not regard it as important—it is all important—but because the personal guaranties are of the highest importance. They constitute a Bill of Rights, a bill of individual rights, of your rights and my rights. These rights are clearly defined and carefully guarded.

I heard a man say the other day that the Constitution ought to be abolished, that it was an obstacle to human progress.[1] He did not say why. That is the trouble with a lot of people in this world; they are ever ready to destroy, but are never ready to aid in building up. Their purpose is destruction, not construction. You will hear a great deal of complaint about the Constitution. I have heard complaint about the Constitution. This is our Constitution. We are directly interested in defending it against all attacks if it is a good thing for us. If it is a bad thing we are all interested in having it repealed. And of course you now fully understand that the people have the power to repeal every line of the Constitution if they want to.[2]

So this morning I wish to submit to you a fair question. *What is there in the Constitution that you think should be taken out of the Constitution? What is there that should be repealed?* I do not ask you to answer that question now. I want you to think it over carefully. Go over each and every word of the Constitution carefully. Talk it over with your father and your mother. Talk it over with your friends, the boys and girls who are studying this subject with you, and some day present to your teacher or to me a statement of the part of the Constitution that you think ought to be repealed. Of course, to come to a just conclusion on this question you must not only look at the language of the Constitution but you must take into consideration the purpose of each provision of the Constitution. That is why we have been studying the Constitution in detail. That is why we have considered in a general way something of the problems of the human race under the past governments of the world. It is after all a simple question—what is good for the people, and what is not good for the people. What is good for *all* the people—not for any special class. The Constitution has been in existence, most of it, for considerably more than a hundred years. During that more than one hundred years what a wonderful development there has been in this country, development not alone in property and in wealth, because after all that is not the main thing, but development in human opportunity! What a wonderful expansion there has been of human rights! What a splendid example we have had of the maintenance and protection of human liberty! What wonderful legislation has been enacted by the people during those years to make life easier for the average man![3]

Consider all these things and then say frankly whether or not any provision of the Constitution should be taken out. In other words, would the repeal of any single personal guaranty, which we have been considering in these lessons, help men, women, and children? Would it make life easier? Would human liberty be better protected? Would the objects of government, the right to life, liberty, and the pursuit of happiness, be more effective?

The Constitution is a sacred document, but there is nothing more sacred than the right to life and liberty and happiness. Therefore do not hesitate to deal fearlessly with the Constitution, but deal with it reverently. It was intended as an aid to humanity. If it does not serve that purpose it should be abolished. If any provision of the Constitution is not an aid to humanity in America let us repeal that provision. Be fearless; be also cautious. Be careful in any change to avoid the ills which we have, that we do not invite other and more grievous ills that we know not of.

The American people owe to themselves, to their children, and to their country, the solemn duty to give earnest consideration to our Constitution. They owe the solemn duty, if the Constitution is serving a great purpose for the people of America, to defend it against all those who may attack. They owe the duty to uphold it and to guard it. It is a sacred trust and this trust cannot be executed except through intelligence, earnestness, patriotism, and loyalty.

Therefore, if there be defects in the Constitution, pick them out and let us unite in removing them, because the cause of humanity is greater than the cause of fidelity to any law or constitution ever enacted by the people.

NOTES AND COMMENTS

1. On December 2, 1917, in New York City, in a meeting of men who called themselves Bolshevists and I. W. W.'s, the following paragraph was an introduction to a set of resolutions drawn up: "We are the Bolshevists of America. We denounce governments, institutions and society; we hail social revolution and the destruction of the existing order of things."

In the preamble to the Constitution of the Independent Workers of the World (I. W. W.) we find this statement: "The working class and the employing class have nothing in common. Between these two classes the struggle must go on, until the workmen of the world organize as a class, take possession of the earth and the machinery of production, and abolish the wage system. Our motto is—*The abolition of the wage system*."

How foolish is the above statement that the working class and the employing class have nothing in common. The truth of the matter is that they have everything in common. Every employer—almost without exception—was once a workman. He was a successful workman, therefore he became more than a workman—he became an employer. Furthermore, workmen cannot exist without employment. Neither can employers exist without the workmen. They are not only each concerned in the welfare of the other; neither can exist without the other.

The following is another passage taken from the resolutions drawn up by the Bolshevists in which they say the general strike is their weapon of defense: "We will strike for a six hour day, then for a four hour day, then for a two hour day, with increased wages all the time, and then we will be strong enough to take everything and work no more."

We wonder how any sensible man can believe such logic as this. Was it not Saint Paul who said that if any man would not work neither should he eat.

The Socialist party platform of 1912 declared in favor of the abolition of the United States Senate, the amendment of the Constitution of the United States by a majority vote of the people, the election of judges for short terms of office, the denial of the right of the U. S. Supreme Court to declare the acts of Congress void.

2.   Article V of the Constitution of the United States provides for the amendment of that fundamental law of the country. It says amendments may be proposed by a bill for amendment being introduced into either house of Congress and passing each house by a two-thirds vote, or secondly, by the State legislatures of two-thirds of the States demanding that Congress call a national convention in which amendments may be proposed. If these proposed amendments are ratified by the legislatures of three-fourths of the States or by conventions called in three-fourths of the States, they become an integral part of th Constitution.

3.   Some of this good legislation includes: Child Labor Laws; Workmen's Compensation Laws; Industrial Insurance for Workingmen; Compulsory Education; Pure Food Laws; Better Sanitary Conditions in Factories; Safety Appliances; Free Medical Inspection for School Children; and Care of the Poor.

ELEMENTARY QUESTIONS

1.   Why are we interested in the Constitution?
2.   Why should we defend it from all attacks?
3.   In what way can we best defend the Constitution?
4.   Why should we wish to modify it?
5.   Just how can the Constitution be modified?
6.   What should be the spirit in which we should enter upon the consideration of amendments to the Constitution?
7.   Just what should be the argument for any changes?
8.   Make a list of some of the modifications you think should be made.
9.   Arrange a debate on each one of these.

ADVANCED QUESTIONS

A.   What is the fallacy of the I. W. W. constitution?
B.   How would you meet their argument?
C.   List the standards which should be used to measure the worth of any suggestion of amendments to the Constitution.
D.   Discuss the process by which former amendments have been made.
E.   Write a paper on any amendments which you think should be adopted to take anything out of the Constitution.

XXV

AMENDING THE CONSTITUTION

THE POWER OF THE PEOPLE—WHAT PROVISIONS SHOULD BE ADDED TO IT

This morning we are going to apply another test to the Constitution of the United States. I have already asked you to analyze and study the Constitution carefully, each provision of the Constitution, to see if there be any portion that should be taken out. This morning I am going to ask you to study the Constitution with a view of determining what, if anything, you wish added to the Constitution. Do not assume that I am imposing a duty which should only be undertaken by some learned lawyer or statesman. This Constitution is a Constitution of the whole people and it must be upheld and defended, not only by lawyers, judges, and public officials, but by the people in every walk of life, by the children as well as by fathers and mothers, by the poor as well as the rich.[1] Therefore I come to you who are children to-day but who in a few short years will be making the laws of this country through your votes at the ballot box. I ask you to decide not only what, if anything, should be taken out of the Constitution, but I ask what, if anything, should be added to the Constitution; and again I want you to form your own opinions about this after a careful study, after conference with your parents and with your friends. It is a strange thing that we seldom hear any one talking to his neighbor about the Constitution. People when they get together talk about all sorts of things, serious and frivolous, but you seldom hear them discussing the gravest problem in human life, which is human government. Do not be afraid to take up the subject with your friends. Do not be afraid to discuss with your friends some provision of the Constitution. You are having a special advantage in being able to study the Constitution while many of your neighbors never had such an opportunity.[2]

What can we add to the Constitution which will make it more effective as an instrument in the protection of life, liberty, and property for us here in America?

Remember, we the American people can add anything to the Constitution that we wish. Nineteen amendments to the Constitution have already been adopted by the people. Do not feel discouraged because it takes a little time to secure the adoption of an amendment. The Constitution should not be amended hastily, but only after grave thought and earnest consideration.

If we can only think of something to add to the Constitution which would be a good thing for the whole people of America, I will guarantee that we will have no difficulty in having it added to the Constitution. Of course it will take earnest effort, but shaping the destiny of more than 105,-000,000 people is a grave matter. The Constitution is the protection of the rights of each individual and therefore any change in the Constitution merits most earnest consideration upon the part of each one of us.

Think it over and advise me some day or inform your teacher of anything that you can think of which, if added to the Constitution, would improve this Nation as a country in which the people rule, anything which would make the rule of the people more complete. That is the big thing after all —the rule of the people, because when the people can rule themselves, they ought to get out of life everything which they are entitled to by their individual merits, ability, and effort. Always keep in mind that there is no way by which a government of the people and by the people can equalize opportunity for those who will not seek the advantages which are open to them. No Constitution and no law can equalize industry and idleness. No scheme of government can provide bread for those who will not toil. It is impossible that human happiness can be guaranteed to those whose lives are spent in wickedness and wrongdoing.

So, my friends, after due thought and deliberation, prepare your amendments to the Constitution of your country. Do not hesitate because you may think that you cannot put them in proper form. The form is not important; the idea is the great thing. Perhaps it may be that out of the mind and out of the heart of some pupil in this school may come some day a great idea which, incorporated into the Constitution or the law, may bring added blessings to the American people.[3] I know of no power on earth which can tie the hands of the American people in any effort toward enlarging the powers of the people, which will better guard life and liberty. We have seen how many safeguards were adopted by the framers of the Constitution to protect each and everyone of us against the abuse of power by the government maintained by the people. We have seen how earnestly the framers of the Constitution guarded each individual against wrongful conduct on the part of any servant of the people in any official position. *Perhaps some one in this class may discover an additional guaranty which would be helpful. If so, duty demands that the same shall be made part of the fundamental laws of our country, the Constitution of the United States.*

As you read of America, as you think of its Constitution and laws, don't you feel a sense of power, a sense of pride?

If Mr. Allen who owns the big department store on Main Street were to come here some morning and make each one of you a gift of an interest in his store, if he should make you partners with him in his entire business, you would feel grateful and proud. What an intense interest you would take in the store and all the details. You would talk about it at home and to your neighbors and friends. Each of you would begin to study the business. You would take pleasure in reading about merchandise, prices, and business methods.

Well, we are all partners in this great Nation. Liberty is more valuable than merchandise or profits. If someone stronger than you should undertake to take away your liberty, you would fight for it and die for it if necessary.

Being partners in America, won't you study America? Won't you talk about the blessings of America at home and to your neighbors? Won't you study the problems of America so that each succeeding year it can pay greater profits in freedom and justice and righteousness?

NOTES AND COMMENTS

1. If you read carefully the fifth article of the Constitution of the United States, you will learn that the Constitution may be amended either by the people's representatives who sit in Congress, and in State legislatures, or by the legislatures of the States demanding that a National convention shall be called in which the people may choose the members. Which ever method of amending the Constitution is used, it is the people who exercise the power of changing the Constitution.

2. Every teacher in every public school ought to feel in duty bound to teach the fundamental principles of the Constitution to all the children in the school. A recitation period ought to be set aside each day for the study of civics of the community, of the locality, of the State, and of the United States. Every pupil in every public school ought to feel proud of the opportunity to learn how his government is made and how his government works, how he may become a helpful citizen by being an intelligent voter when he comes to be a man. Adult people ought to organize civic clubs in the community for the discussion and study of questions of government and politics.

3. The following suggestions have been made by good, honest people who have their country's welfare at heart. Thus far the people as a whole have not advocated their adoption, but some of them may be made part of the Constitution in time to come.

a. The direct popular election of President and Vice President of the United States.

b. The adoption of the initiative, referendum, and recall in the National government.

c. Federal legislation governing both marriage and divorce throughout the Nation.

d. Federal jurisdiction over all cases affecting foreigners—for example in instances like the Italian riot in New Orleans, or in the Japanese problem on the Pacific coast.

ELEMENTARY QUESTIONS

1. What do your parents say about changes in our Constitution?
2. How would you advise them to act?
3. Can you tell them how changes in our Constitution can be made?
4. Why is it necessary that each one of us take a personal interest in OUR Constitution?

ADVANCED QUESTIONS

A. How would you meet the argument of the radical who wants a revolution?
B. How would you show others that we have a great partnership in America?
C. What two ways are possible for constitutional amendments?
D. List a series of additions that you think should be made to the Constitution.
E. Write a paper upon some one amendment to our Constitution that you believe to be worthy of adoption.

XXVI

MACHINERY OF THE GOVERNMENT

THE AGENCIES, OFFICERS, AND METHODS FOR EXERCISING
POWERS OF THE NATIONAL GOVERNMENT

Now my friends, we have reached the end of discussion of the personal guaranties of the Constitution—the American Bill of Rights.

As I have heretofore stated, this is the real, important part of the Constitution, because it is in a study of these guaranties that we fully realize the blessings of our free American government. Any one who has earnestly considered this great American Bill of Rights can readily answer the question, "What has America done for me and for my children"?

But I would not have you feel that the other parts of the Constitution are of small concern. Each provision of this great charter of human rights is very important, and worthy of careful study.

Article I of the Constitution provides that all legislative powers granted "shall be vested in a Congress of the United States, which shall consist of a Senate and House of Representatives". Now you will understand of course that up to the time the Constitution was adopted, the United States had no power; in fact there was no United States. The colonists through the Articles of Confederation had attempted to establish a Nation which was designated "The United States of America", but the result of their efforts was really a confederation, and not a real union.[1] *The Nation was formed by the adoption of the Constitution.* The Nation formed was in the nature of a partnership. I suppose you know but little about partnerships organized by individuals. A partnership is generally formed by a written agreement signed by the partners. This agreement usually contains provisions as to the share or interest of each partner, the power of the partners and of the partnership, and the objects and purposes of the partnership.

The United States is a partnership between the people and the Nation. The Constitution is a partnership agreement binding upon all the parties to the agreement. Before the adoption of the Constitution the people possessed all the power of government and governmental action. The people gave some of their power to the Nation, but only a small part of the power of the people was given. Always bear in mind that the United States—the Nation—has no power, and never had any except what the people granted in the Constitution and in the amendments thereto.

You will see in Section 8 of Article I the specific powers granted to Congress by the people. They include the following: lay and collect taxes; pay debts; provide for defense and for the general welfare; borrow money; regulate commerce among the States and with foreign nations; provide for naturalization and uniform rules of bankruptcy; coin money, regulate the value thereof, and fix the standard of weights and measures; punish counterfeiting; establish post offices and post roads; protect authors and inventors by copyrights and patents; establish courts; punish piracies and felonies on the high seas; declare war, raise, and support armies; provide and maintain a navy; provide for organizing armies, for disciplining the militia, and for calling them to serve in certain emergencies; exercise exclusive power of legislation "over such District (not exceeding ten miles square) as may, by Cession of particular States, and the acceptance of Congress, become the Seat of the Government of the United States"; make all laws necessary and proper for carrying into execution the foregoing powers "and all other Powers vested by this

Constitution in the Government of the United States, or in any Department or Officer thereof."

So you see large powers were granted by the people to the new Nation.

However, the people were very careful. Nearly every government in the world, before the organization of the United States, had at times proven false to the people. Many governments were false to the people all the time. Indignities and abuses were often heaped upon helpless men, women, and children. Governments were more often maintained to serve royalty or aristocracy than to protect the rights and liberties of the common people. Therefore when it came to organizing this new Nation, the people were careful to guard against the abuses of the past. Thus they not only specified definitely the powers conferred upon the United States, but (Sections 9 and 10 of Article I) positively stated certain things which the United States could not do.

The people also were suspicious. The experience of the human race with governments justified this suspicion. When the Constitution was submitted to the people, many protested that the individual liberties of the people were not sufficiently guarded; and before the people consented to ratify the Constitution, it was necessary that they should be given assurance that upon the ratification of the Constitution, amendments would be proposed and submitted to the people, expressing clearly the guaranties given to the people against improper exercise of power by the National government and especially protecting the liberty of all the people. These amendments, which constitute the Great American Bill of Rights, were proposed by Congress in 1789 and were ratified by the States in 1791.

Now let us get the foregoing brief summary fixed in our minds.

The Constitution is a partnership agreement between the

people and the Nation in which the people (1) grant to the Nation certain specific powers; (2) restrain the Nation from exercising powers not granted; and (3) in many particulars direct the manner in which the powers granted shall be exercised. The Constitution also provides for what may be termed the "machinery of government". It separates the powers of government into three divisions: the legislative, the executive, and the judicial. It then provides for the officers (the agents or servants of the people), who shall exercise the powers of each department, and prescribes certain qualifications for such officers, the methods of their selection, and the terms of such officers.

In Article I we find certain qualifications for Senators and Representatives—the length of their term of service. Senators are elected for six years, Representatives for two years. There are also certain provisions as to their election, the organization of the Senate and House, to some extent the method of procedure, and direction as to the exercise of certain powers.

Article II of the Constitution fixes certain qualifications for President of the United States, the executive head of the Nation; provides the manner of the election of the President and the Vice President, confers certain powers and duties, provides that the term of office of President and Vice President shall be four years, and designates the causes for which they may be removed by impeachment.

Article III of the Constitution provides for courts and judges, and fixes their jurisdiction—their power—and gives direction as to trial and penalty in certain cases.

Thus we find that the Constitution guarantees a National government (a republican form of government), confers certain powers formerly held by the people, provides an executive to enforce the powers granted, a legislative body to make laws under which the powers may be exercised, and establishes courts to construe and apply the laws enacted, to the end that human rights and liberties shall be protected.

Let us carry in our minds this picture of the people of the colonies, who through generations had struggled with royalty to secure the blessings and liberties for which they had come to the New World. In the local government of the colonies much had been done to apply the principles of liberty, but in their relation to the mother country they had endured abuses and sufferings, which finally in 1776 found expression in the Declaration of Independence.

In an effort to unite their strength they had formed a federation of the thirteen States, but their dreams of a free country were not realized until in the Constitution they had formed the "more perfect Union" which was created to "establish Justice, insure domestic Tranquility, provide for the common defence, promote the general Welfare, and secure the Blessings of Liberty to ourselves and our Posterity".

Now let us bear in mind that the people reserved much of their power, which under the plan of government adopted was to be used in their respective States under Constitutions and laws expressing the will of the people with relation to their domestic affairs. At our next meeting, we shall consider briefly something of the Constitutions of the States, where they come from, and the wonderful purpose they serve in carrying out the scheme of the people in actual self government.

NOTES AND COMMENTS

1. The following is a brief outline of the various attempts at union among the colonies.
- (a)   1643-1684—New England Confederation: Massachusetts Bay; Plymouth; Connecticut; New Haven.
- (b)   1684—Albany Council.
- (c)   1690—First Colonial Congress.
- (d)   1696—William Penn's Plan.
- (e)   1701—Robert Livingston's Plan.
- (f)   1722—Plan of Daniel Cox.
- (g)   1754—Plan of Rev. Mr. Peters.
- (h)   1754—Plan of the Lords of Trade.

(i)   1754—Albany Plan.
(j)   1765—Stamp Act Congress.
(k)   1774—First Continental Congress.
(l)   1775—Second Continental Congress.
(m)   1781—Congress of the Confederation.
(n)   1787—The Federal Convention.
(o)   1789—The New Government.

The chief reasons keeping the colonies apart were:
1.   Natural geographical divisions—North, Middle, and South.
2.   The great differences in size—Virginia many times larger than Rhode Island.
3.   The instinct of local self government.
4.   Character of settlers and the motives in making settlements.
5.   The slave question, especially after 1750.
6.   Their different forms of government—Royal, Proprietary, Charter.

The very first attempt at constitution making in the colonies was the Mayflower Compact, adopted on board the ship Mayflower before landing on December 20, 1620. It reads as follows: "We, whose names are underwritten, the loyal subjects of our dred soveraigne King James, by the grace of God, of Great Britain, France and Ireland King, defender of the faith, etc. having undertaken, for the glory of God, and advancement of Christian faith and honor of our king and country, a voyage to plant the first colony in northern parts of Virginia, do, by these presents, solemnly and mutually, in the presence of God, and of one another, covenant and combine ourselves together into a civil body politic, for, our better ordering and preservation and furtherance of the ends aforesaid; and, by virtue hereof, to enact, constitute, and frame, such just and equal laws, ordinances, acts, constitutions and offices, from time to time, as shall be thought most meet and convenient for the general good of the colony. Unto which we promise all due submission and obedience. In witness whereof we have hereunder subscribed our names, at Cape Cod, the 11th of November, in the year of the reign of our sovereign lord, King James, of England, France and Ireland the eighteenth, and of Scotland the fifty-fourth, Anno Domini."

The first real attempt at formal constitution making was the "Fundamental Orders of Connecticut", 1639. These "Orders" formed an elementary constitution with three departments of government and the duties and powers of each department fairly well set forth. The Fundamental Orders are frequently referred to as the first written constitution in America.

The Articles of Confederation were made by the *thirteen States* in the name of the *States*. The Constitution was made by the *delegates of the people* in the name of the *people of the United States*. The first was a *compact* or friendly agreement; the second was a *contract* or binding union.

ELEMENTARY QUESTIONS

1.   Why are the individual guaranties of the Constitution so important?
2.   What is meant by legislative power?
3.   In whom is the legislative power of the United States vested?
4.   When and how was the Nation formed?
5.   What is a partnership? How is it usually formed?
6.   From whom did the United States obtain its power?

7. State the terms of service of: (a) the President, (b) Senators, (c) Representatives, (d) the Vice President?

ADVANCED QUESTIONS

A. Tell some of the powers conferred by the people upon the United States.

B. Into what departments does the Constitution separate the powers of government?

C. At the time of the adoption of the Constitution, why were the people suspicious?

D. Name some officers now in service of the National government: (a) in the executive department, (b) in the legislative department, (c) in the judicial department.

E. Write a statement of the attitude of the people of the States when the Constitution was submitted to them for ratification, what was the subject of public discussion, what parties were formed, and what was done to secure the consent of the people to ratify the Constitution?

F. Write in 100 words or less a summary of what the United States Constitution is.

XXVII

STATE CONSTITUTIONS

THE GRANT AND LIMITATIONS OF POWER EXPRESSED BY THE PEOPLE IN THE CONSTITUTIONS OF THE STATES

Every human organization had a beginning. This is a large city in which we now live, but there was a time within the memory of men still living, when there was nothing here but an unbroken prairie. A log cabin was the first building where the city now stands. Then came the cultivated fields. A flour mill was erected down on the river bank, then a blacksmith shop, a store, a livery stable, some modest dwellings, then a school house, and a church. Thus came the little village which through the years has slowly grown into the present city.

Thus came all the cities, and thus came the States. There was a time not so long ago when there were no white people within what is now the borders of our State. There was the "first white settler", the first cultivated patch of ground, the first log house, the little settlements, the lonely log cabins in between, and then the State.

Thus were the thirteen colonies founded, and thus were founded the thirty-five States which have been admitted to the Union since the adoption of the Constitution.

Every human organization with any degree of permanence has something in the nature of a constitution. It may be in writing, it may be oral, or it may rest in a mutual understanding expressed only by acts and conduct. It may be manifest from customs which have been observed by all the members of the group.

The proud boast of America is that it was the first Nation in the world which adopted a complete written Constitution binding upon the Nation and upon the people, a Constitution which provides for courts with the power of restraining the Nation and the individual from acts or conduct which violate its provisions, designed to guard human rights.

Until the Declaration of Independence in 1776, the colonies in their joint efforts for liberty and justice, were called the "United Colonies"; but after independence was proclaimed, this title gave place to that of "The United States". Thereupon eleven of the thirteen States adopted Constitutions. In two States—Connecticut and Rhode Island—by an act of the legislature, the existing charters were continued in force so far as consistent with independence. These Constitutions all came into being before the adoption of the Constitution of the United States. Of course they were far from perfect, and all have been amended from time to time, so that now the Constitution of each State provides a truly American system of government.[1]

Nothing in the Constitution of the United States requires that each State shall have a written Constitution, but the wonderful achievement of the people in creating the Constitution of the United States has been a guide and inspiration to the people of the States, and each State has adopted a written State Constitution, following the method and spirit of the colonists in the long ago, drafting the Constitution in a convention of delegates and ratifying it by another special convention or by the vote of all the people.

Then as each new State was admitted to the Union, a Constitution was adopted.[2] By the Constitution of the United States, Congress has the power to admit new States, thus by implication controlling the subject matter of the original Constitution of each State admitted.

It is not my intention to consider in detail the Constitutions of the various States. This is not essential to the purpose which I have in talking to you. I am very anxious that you shall realize that each State is a separate sovereignty; that when the people created the United States, and adopted the Constitution of the United States, they give to the United States limited power; that the plan of government contemplated that each State should have its own Constitution; and that in each State the people should enact their own laws governing the conduct of the people in their respective States.

An examination of the Constitutions of all the States will show how carefully the people of each State incorporated in their State Constitution the great principles of government, and the guaranties of liberty which were so carefully provided in the Constitution of the United States.

Different language is used in the different State Constitutions, but in each it will be found that the government of the State, as of the United States, is divided into three departments—the executive, the legislative, and the judicial; that the executive power in the States is vested in a Governor; that the legislative power rests in what is usually termed a "General Assembly" consisting of a Senate and a House of Representatives, modeled after the Congress of the United States; that the judicial power is to be exercised by courts—a Supreme Court and other courts designated as District Courts, Circuit Courts, and many other titles, varying in different States.

Public officers, servants of the people, are provided for, and usually their selection is by vote of the people at general elections for which provision is made.

The really important thing in the State Constitutions, as well as in the Constitution of the United States, is the Bill of Rights specifically guarding the natural rights and liberties of the people.

The guaranties in the State Constitutions are not all uniform, but as a general thing you will find that each State has incorporated in its Constitution those sacred guaranties which in the Constitution of the United States form the real foundation and protection of human liberty.

Always bear in mind that the Constitution in each State, as in the Nation, is an instrument of fundamental law, or body of laws, which prescribes the form of government, fixes the different departments of government, provides the agencies of government, and declares and guarantees the rights and liberties of the people.[3]

The Constitution of the United States is the Supreme law of the land, and the Constitution of each State is the supreme law of the State. These Constitutions must be respected, and must be obeyed; and any law enacted by the legislature of a State or by the Congress of the United States which is contrary to the provisions of the Constitution is null and void.

By their Constitution the people of a State proclaim and establish their power superior to the power of the legislature of the State or any officer of the State. The power expressed in the Constitution is the power of the people. They have, by their solemn document—the Constitution—established certain rules, regulations, principles, and guaranties, which cannot be changed by ordinary legislation.[4] Of course the people can change and modify the Constitution of State or Nation. Every Constitution provides some method of amendment. Some States provide for a constitutional convention from time to time, where the people through their representatives selected for such a purpose assemble to consider the question of change or modification. In other States the legislature may propose amendments which must be submitted to the people for their approval. In all States some procedure is provided which requires careful deliberation and consideration by the people before the Constitution is changed.[5]

Now it is very important that every citizen shall have a knowledge of the Constitution of his State. It is of the highest importance that every man, woman, and child shall know and feel the solicitude, the care, which has been exercised in the framing of the Constitution to guard individual rights.

As I have heretofore explained, the purpose of government is to guard human rights and human liberty. This is true of the government of the United States, and it is true of the government of each State. Always keep in mind that in this country, what we call "the government" is merely an agency of the people—an expression of the power of the people in a defined way, agreed upon by them, through which they protect themselves against wrong by the agencies of government which they have created, and against wrong by their neighbors.

Inspiring indeed is it to contemplate the spirit in which the founders of the American Nation and of the States of America studied the methods by which human rights should be protected. They were unselfish; they were in the highest degree inspired by a holy purpose to guard the people of America against the wrongs, the abuses, the cruelty which their ancestors in the past had suffered; and to accomplish their purpose they exercised the greatest care to maintain the power of government in the people themselves—the power to make laws and to enforce them.

I suppose it may be said that the highest achievement of the American people in creating a National government and the governments of the States is expressed in the words of Lincoln when he proclaimed this to be "a government by the people".

NOTES AND COMMENTS

1. Great modifications have been made in nearly all of the State Constitutions, an excellent analysis of which may be found in Bryce's *American Commonwealth* (Third Edition), Vol. I, p. 443.

2. Since the alliance of the original thirteen States, thirty-five have been admitted into the Union by acts of Congress either directing the people to select delegates and enact a Constitution or accepting a Constitution already made by the people. An illustration of the former method of procedure is offered in 25 U. S. St. at L. 676 c 180, providing for the admission of North Dakota, South Dakota, Montana, and Washington into the Union, and of the latter in 26 U. S. St. at L. 215 c 656;

222 c 664, providing for the admission of Idaho and Wyoming. "Of these instruments (State Constitutions), therefore, no less than of the Constitutions of the thirteen original States, we may say that although subsequent in date to the Federal Constitution, they are, so far as each state is concerned de jure prior to it. Their authority over their own citizens is nowise derived from it".—Bryce's *American Commonwealth* (Third Edition), Vol. I, p. 431.

3. "A constitution is an instrument of government, made and adopted by the people for practical purposes, connected with the common business and wants of human life. For this reason pre-eminently every word in it should be expounded in its plain, obvious and common sense".—Per Allen J., in Peo v. New York Cent. R. Co., 24 *N. Y.* 485, 486.

4. Legislatures cannot change Constitutions. "I consider the people of this country as the only sovereign power. I consider the legislature as not sovereign, but subordinate; they are subordinate to the great constitutional charter, which the people have established as a fundamental law and which alone has given existence and authority to the legislature."—Per Roane, J. in Kanper v. Hawkins, 1 *Va. Cas.* 20, 36.

5. "Some of the state constitutions provide for periodically submitting to the voters the question whether a convention shall be called to revise and amend the constitution. Regardless of whether or not provision is made for periodical resubmission of the question of calling a convention, the constitutions usually provide that the legislature may, of its own volition, submit to a vote of the people the question whether a convention shall be called, and subject to any existing constitutional limitations, may prescribe the time and manner of electing delegates to such convention."

ELEMENTARY QUESTIONS

1. What is a village?
2. What is a State?
3. When were the colonies first called States?
4. What States adopted Constitutions before the adoption and ratification of the Constitution of the United States?
5. Can the people of the State of New York enact a law punishing a person for coining silver dollars? Why?
6. Can Congress pass a law fixing the punishment of a person for stealing a horse in the State of Michigan?
7. When was the State in which we live admitted to the Union?
8. Who framed the Constitution of this State?

ADVANCED QUESTIONS

A. What is a constitution?
B. Explain fully how a Constitution of a State comes into being.
C. Must a constitution be in writing? If not, what may be its form?
D. State how the Constitution of the United States may be amended.
E. In what way may the Constitution of a State be amended?
F. Write briefly telling the advantages of a written constitution.
G. State in writing the power of the courts in exercising their power and duty of defending the Constitution. Give an illustration.
H. Write an explanation of the power and influence of the Constitution of the United States in guiding the people in framing the Constitutions of their States, and in what things the Constitutions of the States follow the Constitution of the United States.

XXVIII

THE SUFFRAGE

THE SIGNIFICANCE OF THE NINETEENTH AMENDMENT TO THE CONSTITUTION

This meeting was at night. Some of the parents who had attended the talks from time to time had requested that the last meeting be held at night so that some of the busy fathers and mothers might come. The assembly room was crowded, and although extra chairs had been placed in the aisles, there were a number of people standing. The principal said that it was the largest crowd that he had ever seen in the room.[1]

First everybody arose and sang "The Star Spangled Banner", and when the meeting closed, the audience joined in singing "America".[2] The judge was greeted with loud applause. He said:

I am happy to-night. This meeting is an inspiration. It is a real community meeting, a real American meeting. If meetings like this were held once each week or once every two weeks in every school building in the United States I should not fear socialism or bolshevism or anarchy. Such ideas cannot live in a community where the people really know each other. There are no class lines here to-night. You are too close together. I see a banker over there whom I have known for thirty years. He was brought up in this city, attended this school, and has spent his whole life here. His success in life came to him among old friends in the community where he was born. Near him I see a bricklayer. I have known him and respected him since boyhood. We played on the same baseball team when we were both younger and could run faster than we can now. He went to the Washington school. The children of these men are in this school now. In a few years they will be grown men and women doing the work that we shall have to give up soon.[3]

So with most of the people in this room to-night. They were born here, went to school here, and they have worked here all their lives. Some followed one occupation, some another. This was a matter of their own choice. Their children are now growing up, as they once grew up. Soon they will be selecting their life work. Soon they will be voting and performing other duties of citizenship. Soon you and I, fathers and mothers, will pass off the stage of life. Soon we shall be forgotten by all except the few who compose the family circle, who love us notwithstanding our faults.

For a few weeks I have been acting as teacher. I have been trying hard to bring into the minds and hearts of the pupils in this school something of the sacredness of human liberty, something of the cost of American liberty, the sacrifices, the struggles, the bloodshed, the heartaches, and heartbreaks which finally triumphed when our Constitution was adopted. I have endeavored to explain that the Constitution is not a mere skeleton or framework, defining the relation of the Nation and the States and providing for the election of officers to carry out the plans of the National government. I have repeatedly told the great truth that in America there is more freedom, justice, charity, and kindness than in any other Nation in the world. I have pointed out that in America we have in our Constitution written guaranties of life, liberty, and property rights such as no other Nation in the history of the world ever had. We have found that this is a government by the people, that the people rule, that the few cannot rule unless the many refuse to perform their duties as citizens of this great republic. Oh! if we can only put in the hearts of the American people a realization of the *power* and the *duty* of the people!

To-night I wish to present briefly something of the manner

in which the people express their power, the method by which the people disclose their wishes in public affairs. The Star Baseball Club, the Irving Literary Society, the City Teachers Association, the Woman's Club, the Charity Guild, these are all mere organizations of people. *That is all that America is.* These organizations have written constitutions. *So has America.* These organizations must have laws or rules of conduct, aside from their constitutions. *So must America.* These societies must have a policy and transact business. *So must America.* In adopting laws or rules of conduct these societies secure an expression of the wishes of their members. These wishes are generally expressed by their votes, somtimes by ballot and sometimes orally in a meeting.

America secures an expression of the wishes of the people by their votes. The votes of the people either in writing or printed are cast on election days fixed by laws enacted through the vote of the people. In no other way can the wishes of the people be made known. It is through the ballot that the people exercise their powers. It is through the ballot that America is governed.[4]

I wonder if the people of America generally realize what a wonderful thing it is that a government as large as ours must depend entirely upon the wishes of the people expressed by their vote on election day. I wonder if they realize that in this way the people rule. On election day we see something of the equality of the people. If you go near the polling place, you will see the president of the bank, perhaps, or the president of the railroad walking side by side with the hodcarrier or the brakeman on the train. In the voting booth each has the same power in helping to shape the destiny of their country.

In a way this is a new method of government. Only in a country where there is a government by the people do we find such a thing as the right of all men regardless of property, race, or creed to exercise the same power in the ballot box.[5]

From the beginning America has led in granting the right of suffrage, the right to vote. In the early days in some of the States a man had to own a certain amount of property before he could vote, but this has not been true for more than fifty years. *Now a new day has come.* After a struggle for generations, the right to vote has been conferred upon all female citizens, regardless of property, social position, religion, or race. It has been a long struggle and now that victory has been won for equal suffrage, is there anyone who will still contend that in this country the people do not rule?

Who has conferred this great privilege upon the women of America? The voters of America decided that every State should grant this privilege.

The amendment to the Constitution is as follows:

"The right of citizens of the United States to vote shall not be denied or abridged by the United States or by any State on account of sex."

The people did not vote directly upon this constitutional amendment, but they voted for the members of the House and the members of the Senate who voted for the amendment and they voted for the members of the legislatures of the different States which ratified the amendment. Thus the responsibility rests with the people. This is true of course as to nearly all the laws enacted by State and Nation—the people do not vote directly upon them, but they select their agents, who, under the law, are authorized to act for them.

Under this amendment we have the written guaranty in the Constitution that so far as men and women are concerned they shall have equal rights to vote.[6]

Perhaps you were not in favor of woman suffrage. Many good men and women were opposed to it. Many are still opposed to it. This is a good illustration of the way we do things in a democracy. We have different temperaments, different dispositions. We are reared in different surroundings. We have different interests. We look at life in different ways. Each of us has a right to his opinion and each of us has the right to express it by our vote. When we finally vote, a decision is made. If we belong to the majority, we find that our wish is carried out. If we are in the minority, we cheerfully follow what the majority of the people, what most of the people in America desire.

The thing that I wish to impress to-night is that to vote on election day is not only a right, it is a duty. Whether we were for woman suffrage or not it has come. It is settled. It brings into power twenty-seven million new voters. Each of these women, whether she desires it or not, must assume this new share of the responsibilities of government. It is a patriotic duty. At every election we must cast our votes. Before every election we must study the issues, the problems to be met. Unless we do that we are failing in patriotism and loyalty. Unless we vote we are not good citizens.

Now I must close. I hope that the talks I have given in this school have planted in the hearts of boys and girls, and possibly in the hearts of grown men and women, something of the simple truth of American life, something perhaps of the privileges of American citizenship and something of the duties that we all owe in return.

I have promised the principal of this school that next term I will again appear and present some new topics. I wish to talk to the boys and girls about authority and obedience, the source of authority and the duty of obedience. I wish also to talk about the making of laws, the origin of laws, how they are put in form and finally enacted by the people. I wish to talk about our public servants, because one of the important things for each citizen to know is that from the President of the United States down to the constable of the humblest village, all officers are mere servants of the people and that no officer in America is in his official capacity master of any man, woman, or child. I wish to impress as far as I am able the great truth expressed by Chief Justice Marshall when he said long years ago, "This is a government of laws and not of men."

NOTES AND COMMENTS

1. Teachers and school officers can perform no higher duty, can render no greater service to America, than to encourage the use of school buildings for public gatherings. They should be real community centers. In the city of Minneapolis, the Superintendent of Schools has recently reported that for the year ending July 1st, 1920, there were 5070 meetings held in the public school buildings, with a total attendance of 325,734 persons. There were 1434 cultural meetings, 751 civic sessions, 2501 recreative gatherings, and 334 social festivals. Rural consolidated school buildings ought always be planned for civic centers as well as schoolhouses. They ought to provide a large assembly hall where community gatherings may be held. They ought to provide a large and well equipped gymnasium where both children and adults may enjoy athletic contests and indoor games. These buildings ought to be open to the people every evening during the week if the attendance warrants.

2. One mark of good citizenship is the respect shown to emblems of authority. All good citizens rise to their feet and remain standing during the playing or singing of the National anthem. We ought to cultivate such habits until they become reflex: i. e. until we do them as a matter of course without being told by the teacher in school or by the leader of the choir or some other person.

Every school boy and girl ought to commit to memory the words of the Star Spangled Banner and of America. The teacher can make the singing of patriotic songs and the learning of patriotic poems and speeches a part of the opening exercises of the school. Poems and speeches learned in childhood will generally remain with us throughout life.

3. Radicalism of thought and action can generally be traced to the segregation of the people into small groups where the individual is alone in his thinking. Association and coöperation tend to break up individualism. Where men and women come together in thought and consideration, there is always developed a tendency toward moderation. Our present day complex society demands that every individual yield something for the good of the whole community. The yielding process is a moderating process. Anarchy stands for the division of society into individuals where each individual becomes selfish and dominating over others around him. Loyalty to the Nation and the State requires that the individual shall coöperate with his neighbor and that he shall work in harmony with other people in the community. If people would more often assemble and discuss the needs of the entire community and how each may help to make the entire community better, we would have less of class distinction and more of social harmony and of economic prosperity.

4. Republican government is government by the people through their chosen representatives. Republican government can only be good government and effective government, when every qualified voter will assume

his full duty in helping carry on the government. This duty is exercised through the casting of an intelligent ballot on election day. In the presidential election of 1908 the percentage of qualified voters actually voting ranged from 15.8 per cent to 88.1 per cent, the average for all States being 60.5 per cent.

5. In colonial times in America there was nothing like universal manhood suffrage. One-half of all the colonies required church membership for a suffrage right. By about 1700 all colonies required ownership of property for voting. This was not entirely abolished until about 1850. The State of Rhode Island still requires property to the extent of $134 for voting in municipal elections.

The colony of Virginia required the holding of a freehold of fifty acres of land without a house, or twenty-five acres of land with a house at least twelve feet square. Pennsylvania required a freehold of fifty acres with twelve acres improved.

In most colonies a greater property qualification was required for voting for members of the upper house of the legislature than for members of the lower house.

Several colonies and early States limited office holding to Protestants.

The Constitution of the United States now declares that no State shall deny to any person the right to vote because of *race, color,* or *previous condition of servitude,* or *because of sex.* The Nineteenth Amendment enables women to vote on an equality with men.

A State may add further qualifications for voting, but no State may deny the right to vote for any of the above reasons. Several States have added literacy tests for voting, and others have denied the right to vote to such as are insane or who have been convicted of crime, unless pardoned by the Governor. A few States deny suffrage to those whose taxes are delinquent.

6. The following countries of the world have equal suffrage: New Zealand, 1893; South Australia, 1895: West Australia, 1900; The Australian Federation, 1902; New South Wales, 1902; Tasmania, 1904; Queensland, 1905; Finland, 1906; Victoria, 1908; Alaska, 1913; Norway, 1913; Manitoba, 1916; Alberta, 1916; Iceland, 1913; Denmark, 1915; England, Scotland, Ireland, 1917; Sweden, 1918; Holland, 1919; Luxemburg, 1919; Germany, 1919; Austria, 1919. In no other country in the world is the right of suffrage more fully granted than in the United States since the adoption of the Nineteenth Amendment.

ELEMENTARY QUESTIONS

1. Show the ways in which the United States is just like a small club?
2. Why must we always vote?
3. Why is it right that women should vote?
4. Show that this is more than a privilege: it is a duty.
5. Imagine some person saying that America is only for the rich. Review all the work that we have done, and show how it is just as fair to the poor man as to the rich.

ADVANCED QUESTIONS

A. Re-read the questions to chapters one and two. Note the difference in your answers.
B. Map out a program so that you can show to all critics of America the

ways in which the Constitution of the United States gives to all Americans the rights to LIFE, LIBERTY, and the PURSUIT OF HAPPINESS.

C. You can now answer fully the question, "Why is America the most free and most just Nation on the globe?"

D. What did Chief Justice Marshall mean when he said, "This is a government of laws, and not of men."

E. Prepare in writing a constitution for the "Lincoln Debating Club".

A WORD TO THE TEACHERS AND OTHERS

"The very essence of civil liberty certainly consists in the right of every individual to claim the protection of the laws whenever he receives an injury. One of the first duties of government is to afford that protection. The Government of the United States has been emphatically termed, a government of laws, and not of men. It will certainly cease to deserve this high appellation, if the laws furnish no remedy for the violation of a vested legal right."

These words of Chief Justice Marshall in Marbury v. Madison, 1 Cranch, 137, are the most significant and far reaching in their effect upon human government that were ever uttered by the lips of man.

"A government of laws and not of men." This expresses the fundamental difference between the government of this great American republic and all other systems of government devised by man before the Constitution of the United States came into being.[1]

Government has been the great problem of the human race throughout all the ages since mankind first started out upon the great highway of life. The greatest problem men have ever been called upon to solve is "how they might live together in communities without cutting each others throats".

As we look back at the warring world of yesterday, yea as we look at the warring world to-day (1920), we are reminded that the history of the human family tells a long, sad story of war and bloodshed and death. The path which humanity has traveled stretches back into the dim distance, a long gleaming line of white human bones. The flowers, the trees, and the shrubs along the way have been nurtured by the red blood that flowed from human hearts. All over the world the battle has waged; away down in Egypt where the Nile scatters her riches; upon the banks of the Tiber which for centuries has reflected the majesty of Rome; upon the heights above the castle crowned Rhine; on the banks of the peaceful Thames; and upon the prairies that sweep back from the Father of Waters, men have fought and died. In the field and in the forest, by the sweet running brook, and upon the burning sands, in the mountain pass, and in the stony streets of the populous city, within the chancel rail of holy churches, and at the dark entrance to the Bastile—in all these places, and in a thousand more, the hand of the oppressed has been lifted against the oppressor, the right to be free that God gave to men has struggled with the power which might has given, and, alas! so often might has triumphed, and the slave, sick at heart, has been scourged to his dungeon. On a thousand hillsides burning fagots have consumed men who dared to dream of freedom, and in dark and slimy prison cells where God's sunlight seldom entered, men have rotten with clanking chains upon their limbs because they dared to ask for the rights of freemen.

In the olden days force ruled the world; the king, the crown, the scepter, were the insignia of power. All about were the instruments of force, the cannon, the moated castle, the marching armies of the king.

And so it was until the American Nation was born, a Nation founded by exiles who were fleeing from oppression, from unrestrained power, exiles who dreamed of establishing a Nation, exiles with stout hearts and with strong hands with which to build it—a Nation where there would be no master and no slaves, where the citizen would rule and not the soldier, where the home and the school and not the castle would stand as the citadel of the Nation, where the steel would at last be molded into plowshares, and not into swords, where, instead of martial music, the song of the plowboy and the hum of the spinning wheel would greet the ear, where lust for power would be dethroned and brute force strangled, where love would rule and not brutality, where justice and not vengeance would be the end of judicial investigation, where the rights of men to live and to enjoy the fruits of their labor would be recognized. This was the dream of the fathers of the republic as they laid the foundation in the long ago.

But this dream never would have been realized had it not been for the recognition of that great constitutional principle, anounced by Chief Justice Marshall, that in this Nation the law is supreme; not supreme alone with the citizen, but supreme with the Nation and the States that compose the Nation; not supreme with the humble toiler, but supreme with the richest and the strongest; not supreme in theory, but supreme in truth and in fact.

This great principle of the supremacy of the law finds its origin in that immortal document, the Constitution of the United States.[2]

Few there are in these modern days who fully appreciate the wonderful blessings of a written Constitution which gives recognition to the fundamental natural rights of man, and provides guaranties against the invasion of these rights.

Gladstone, the eminent statesman, said:

It (the American Constitution) is the greatest work ever struck off at any one time by the mind and purpose of man.

An eminent lawyer has said:

It has been the priceless adjunct of free government, the mighty shield of the rights and liberties of the citizen. It has been many times invoked to save him from illegal punishment, and save his property from the greed of unscrupulous enemies, and to save his political rights from the unbridled license of victorious political opponents controlling legislative bodies; nor does it sleep, except as a sword dedicated to a righteous cause sleeps in its scabbard.

Horace Binney says:

What were the States before the Union? The hope of their enemies, the fear of their friends, and arrested only by the Constitution from becoming the shame of the world.

Sir Henry Maine gives the following estimate of the Constitution:

It isn't at all easy to bring home to the men of the present day, how low the credit of the Republic had sunk before the establishment of the United States. . . . . Its success has been so great and striking, that men have almost forgotten, that if the whole, or the known experiments of mankind in governments be looked at together, there has been no form of government so successful as the republican.

Justice Mitchell of Pennsylvania, some twenty odd years ago said:

A century and a decade has passed since the Constitution of the United States was adopted. Dynasties have arisen and fallen, boundaries have extended and shrunken 'till continents seem almost the playthings of imagination and war; nationalities have been asserted and subdued; governments built up only to be overthrown, and the kingdoms of the earth from the Pillars of Hercules to the Yellow Sea have been shaken to their foundations. Through all this change and obstruction, the Republic, shortest lived of all forms of government in the prior history of the world, surviving the perils of foreign and domestic war, has endured and flourished.

And yet, it is true, "and pity 'tis, 'tis true", that in these days there seems to be a great lack of confidence, nay even a feeling of contempt existing in the minds and hearts of many men for this great charter of human liberty. Men born to the blessings of freedom, men who do not stop to think about the cost of freedom, men who do not realize that this Nation is not the child of chance, but that it is the outgrowth of centuries of tears and blood and sacrifice in the cause of human freedom—these men assume an attitude of criticism, and would, by destroying the Constitution, fly from the "ills we have" and open their arms to evils "we know not of".

And this feeling, this unrest, this spirit of criticism, is not limited to the ignorant, nor the lowly. Many men and women of education and culture are prominent in the ranks of those who raise their voices in reckless condemnation.

What is the source of this widespread feeling?

For several years before the World War, we were passing through a period of readjustment in the political and social life of the Nation. Many people felt that privilege was too strongly entrenched in governmental favor. A noble feeling of sympathy for the weak and the unfortunate created a demand for social justice. A great political party was thrown out of power. Out of all this came appeals for legislation, most of it inspired by the highest motives, but much of it impractical and visionary, some of it so framed that in providing a benefit for a certain class, the rights of some other class were forgotten. Often it became necessary to recall the provisions of the Constitution, and some times it was used as a bar to the enactment of measures which were inspired only by the loftiest motives. Under such circumstances it is only natural that those intensely interested, seeing only from one standpoint, not understanding perhaps the far reaching effect of their favorite measures, should cry out at the limitations imposed by the Constitution.

Then again courts are sometimes compelled, under their sworn duty to defend the Constitution, to hold that a legislative enactment is unconstitutional and void, because it violates some of the principles of that great document, created, not by courts, not by presidents, but by the people themselves for their own guidance and protection.

But Chief Justice White gives the strongest reason for this feeling of contempt for the Constitution. He says:

There is great danger, it seems to me, to arise, from the constant habit which prevails where anything is opposed or objected to, of resorting without rhyme or reason, to the Constitution as a means of preventing its accomplishment, thus creating the general impression that the Constitution is but a barrier to progress, instead of being the broad highway through which alone true progress, may be enjoyed.

Not only is this true, but unfortunately it is also true that every base murderer who begins to feel the rope tighten about his neck can find some lawyer who can devise some alleged constitutional reason why his client should not hang. The courts are constantly engaged in defending the Constitution against these base and unworthy attempts to defeat justice.

Then upon every hand are those who hate authority, who despise law and order, and who denounce the Constitution because it stands between them and a realization of their greedy, vicious purposes.

Justice White further says that there is "a growing tendency to suppose that every wrong that exists, despite the system, and which would be many times worse if the system did not exist, is attributable to it, and therefore that the Constitution should be disregarded or over-thrown".

The foregoing are some, but not all of the causes which weaken the faith of the people in the Constitution.

Now recognizing that there is in this Nation a lack of respect for the Constitution, and knowing something of the causes which underlie this feeling, and realizing that the Constitution is in very truth the fortress and the glory of our republic, what is our duty?

The duty of every man, woman, and child in America is to defend the Constitution with his life, if necessary, against those who condemn and traduce and seek to destroy.

But how shall we defend it? Shall we oppose all amendments of the Constitution? No, by its very terms it is subject to amendment; but in contemplating its amendment, we should approach this sacred document in the same reverent spirit we would have if we were entering upon some holy shrine. It is the people's Constitution; it is their right to amend it. Yea, it is their duty to amend it, if upon due deliberation, the rights of the whole people can be better protected or enforced.

Complaint is sometimes made because of the delay involved in its amendment; but the provisions of the Constitution re-

quiring deliberation were wisely inserted. It was intended
that fundamental principles should not be changed under
the inspiration of sudden passion. It contemplated mature
deliberation. The fathers of the Republic were mindful of
the storms which at times in the history of the world had
swept the people to destruction.[3]

Shall we rebuke the people who seek reforms? *Shall we
decry progress or change?* No, we should be the leaders in
all such reforms. We should aid in guiding public sentiment along channels safe and sound and constitutional. We
should give recognition to the appeals of those who would
lighten the burdens of our brothers who may be heavy laden.
We should aid in convincing the people that the Constitution is no restraint upon their aspirations for higher and better things; that it is in truth the guide and inspiration to
better things.

Shall we condemn those who through lack of knowledge
do not appreciate the great value of the Constitution? No,
we should teach them. We should lead them. We should
inspire them with love and veneration for this great bulwark
of human freedom.

We must in very truth become teachers of all the people.
We must carry to them the light of our knowledge. We must
carry to them the light of our knowledge. We must point
out to them the rocks upon which other republics have been
wrecked.[4]

We must teach them that in the Constitution we find an
absolute guaranty of protection for life, for liberty, and for
property rights. That there is no man so lowly, that he cannot
point to the Constitution as his shield from the acts of the
tyrant, that he cannot point to his humble home as his
"castle", and under the sacred guaranties of the Constitution
defy all the unlawful force of the world.

We must teach them that it guarantees the inviolability of

contracts, that it prevents even a great State from taking the life or property of its humblest citizen without a trial under due process of law, that trial by jury is preserved, and that no man can be convicted of a crime without the privilege of being represented by counsel, and that no man can be compelled to be a witness against himself.

We must recall to them the awful tragedies enacted in the days of old, where, under Star Chamber proceedings, men were deprived of their property and their lives upon charges of treason, which were never proven; and then we must point out to them the burning words of the Constitution, which provides that no man can be found guilty of treason without at least two witnesses to the overt act.

We must impress upon them the great truth, that there is not now, and never has been, a system of government which can abolish sorrow, or sickness, or stay the hand of death. That no government can help men who will not help themselves; that there is no way in which any government can bring riches to the indolent, nor bread to those who will not toil. We must combat the false philosophy which assumes that all men are equal in all things, because men are not equal, except as under the Constitution they are equal before the law. No system of legislation and no method of government can equalize the strong with the weak, the wise with the simple, the good with the bad. While God gives to some men wisdom and shrewdness which others do not possess, while some are broad shouldered, with muscles of steel, and others are frail, and tremble as they walk, there will always be riches, there will always be poverty, and any scheme for equalizing the possessions of men is but an idle dream which never can be realized until men are made over into beings without passion or pride or ambition or selfishness. Do not let them feel that its provisions are intended to protect only the rich and powerful. If the right of a railway corporation to certain lands is sustained under some constitutional provision, do not allow the people to assume that this provision exists only for corporations, but impress upon them that the same constitutional provision which protects the railway company in its rights, may be invoked in defense of the little homestead out upon the prairies.

If some desperado should be acquitted because he invoked the constitutional requirement that he upon his trial must be confronted by the witnesses against him, remind those who criticise that this same provision is made for their sons who may to-morrow be unjustly charged with a crime; impress upon them that it is impossible to have one law for the guilty, and another for the innocent; and that under our Constitution, every man is presumed to be innocent until proven to be guilty.

Then impress upon the people something of the wonderful growth of the Nation, the development of the Nation, and the progress of the Nation—all under the wise protection of the Constitution. To those who may be discouraged in the battle of life, and who may attribute their failure to the injustice of social conditions, point out what other men have done under the same conditions, with no better opportunity, and ask them to ponder the question as to whether their failure is not to be attributed largely to their own lack of energy and determination.[5]

And if they point out abuses which do exist, ask them to aid in eliminating these abuses. If half the energy which is exerted by earnest, but misguided people, in efforts to tear down our form of government, were honestly applied in an effort to remedy existing evils in a constitutional way, these people would show that they were patriots, and at the same time they would accomplish something for their country and their fellowmen.[6]

Too long have we been silent while the enemies of our

country have poisoned the minds of youth, yea, and of manhood and womanhood, with the gospel of treason.

Those who despise and condemn the Constitution have in the past ten years had more earnest students of their vicious doctrines than have those who uphold the Constitution and prize their liberties which the Constitution guards and protects.

All over the land earnest men and women are endeavoring to teach the great truth of Americanism, and with substantial success; but those who understand human nature realize that the faith of our fathers can only be firmly established by lighting the fires of patriotism and loyalty in the hearts of our children. Through them the great truths of our National life can be brought into the homes of the land.

And the Nation will never be safe until the Constitution is carried into the homes, until at every fireside young and old shall feel a new sense of security in the guaranties which are found in this great charter of human liberty, and a new feeling of gratitude for the blessings which it assures to this, and to all future generations.

NOTES AND COMMENTS

1. "Any government is free to the people under it (whatever be the frame) where the laws rule and the people are a party to those laws."—William Penn.

2. "It is, Sir, the people's Constitution, the people's government, made for the people, made by the people and answerable to the people."—Daniel Webster.

3. "In truth success cannot be expected from any system of government unless the individuals who compose the State entertain the respect for the personal rights and liberties of all."—David Jayne Hill.

4. "We cannot, we must not, we dare not, omit to do that which, in our judgment, the safety of the Union requires."—Daniel Webster.

5. "Americanization always implies obligation; free choice determines its acceptance, and its extension must come through avenues of intelligent comprehension rather than through physical or governmental domination."—Winthrop Talbot.

6. "The fundamental evil in this country is the lack of sufficiently general appreciation of the responsibility of citizenship."—Theodore Roosevelt.

Teachers of children may well place greater emphasis on *ideals, char-*

acter, and *personality* as factors in the making of a Nation. Teachers ought to lay greater stress on biography in the teaching of history, civics, and citizenship. Teach children both to know and to love Washington, Lincoln, and Roosevelt. Teach older pupils and students to realize that the aims, ideals, and achievements of a Nation can never be higher than the aims, ideals, and achievements of the individuals comprising that Nation. To know the lives and characters of America's great men and women is to know American history, for they made American history what it is. Young people enjoy the study of great characters. We all retain a love for heroes and heroines however old we grow. Such study adds color and life to history and government and humanizes the entire subject. Teach lives and institutions rather than mere facts. Inculcate into the lives of boys and girls, and of men and women, a love for our country, for the men and women who made it, and for the institutions in which they have a part. Teach them that patriotism and loyalty are not duties only, but are rather the highest privileges given to the people of a republic.

DECLARATION OF INDEPENDENCE

When in the Course of human events, it becomes necessary for one people to dissolve the political bands which have connected them with another, and to assume among the Powers of the earth, the separate and equal station to which the Laws of Nature and of Nature's God entitle them, a decent respect to the opinions of mankind requires that they should declare the causes which impel them to the separation.

We hold these truths to be self-evident, that all men are created equal, that they are endowed by their Creator with certain unalienable Rights, that among these are Life, Liberty and the pursuit of Happiness. That to secure these rights, Governments are instituted among Men, deriving their just powers from the consent of the governed. That whenever any form of Government becomes destructive of these ends, it is the Right of the People to alter or abolish it, and to institute new Government, laying its foundation on such principles and organizing its powers in such form, as to them shall seem most likely to effect their Safety and Happiness. Prudence, indeed, will dictate that Governments long established should not be changed for light and transient causes; and accordingly all experience hath shown, that mankind are more disposed to suffer, while evils are sufferable, than to right themselves by abolishing the forms to which they are accustomed. But when a long train of abuses and usurpations, pursuing invariably the same Object evinces a design to reduce them under absolute Despotism, it is their right, it is their duty, to throw off such Government, and to provide new Guards for their future security.— Such has been the patient sufferance of these Colonies; and such is now the necessity which constrains them to alter their former Systems of Government. The history of the present King of Great Britain is a history of repeated injuries and usurpations, all having in direct object the establishment of an absolute Tyranny over these States. To prove this, let Facts be submitted to a candid world.

He has refused his Assent to Laws, the most wholesome and necessary for the public good.

He has forbidden his Governors to pass Laws of immediate and pressing importance, unless suspended in their operation till his Assent should be obtained; and when so suspended, he has utterly neglected to attend to them.

He has refused to pass other Laws for the accommodation of large districts of people, unless those people would relinquish the right of Representation in the Legislature, a right inestimable to them and formidable to tyrants only.

He has called together legislative bodies at places unusual, uncomfortable, and distant from the depository of their Public Records, for the sole purpose of fatiguing them into compliance with his measures.

He has dissolved Representative Houses repeatedly, for opposing with manly firmness his invasion on the rights of the people.

He has refused for a long time, after such dissolutions, to cause others to be elected; whereby the Legislative Powers, incapable of Annihilation, have returned to the People at large for their exercise; the State remaining in the mean time exposed to all the dangers of invasion from without, and convulsions within.

He has endeavoured to prevent the population of these States; for that purpose obstructing the Laws for Naturalization of Foreigners; refusing to pass others to encourage their migration hither, and raising the conditions of new Appropriations of Lands.

He has obstructed the Administration of Justice, by refusing his Assent to Laws for establishing Judiciary Powers.

He has made Judges dependent on his Will alone, for the tenure of their offices, and the amount and payment of their salaries.

He has erected a multitude of New Offices, and sent hither swarms of officers to harass our People, and eat out their substance.

He has kept among us, in times of peace, Standing Armies without the Consent of our legislature.

He has affected to render the Military independent of and superior to the Civil Power.

He has combined with others to subject us to a jurisdiction foreign to our constitution, and unacknowledged by our laws; giving his Assent to their Acts of pretended Legislation:

For quartering large bodies of armed troops among us:

For protecting them, by a mock Trial, from Punishment for any Murders which they should commit on the Inhabitants of these States:

For cutting off our Trade with all parts of the world:

For imposing taxes on us without our Consent:

For depriving us in many cases, of the benefits of Trial by Jury:

For transporting us beyond Seas to be tried for pretended offences:

For abolishing the free System of English Laws in a neighbouring Province, establishing therein an Arbitrary government, and enlarging its Boundaries so as to render it at once an example and fit instrument for introducing the same absolute rule into these Colonies.

For taking away our Charters, abolishing our most valuable Laws, and altering fundamentally the Forms of our Government:

For suspending our own Legislatures, and declaring themselves invested with Power to legislate for us in all cases whatsoever.

He has abdicated Government here, by declaring us out of his Protection and waging War against us.

He has plundered our seas, ravaged our Coasts, burnt our towns, and destroyed the lives of our people.

He is at this time transporting large armies of foreign mercenaries to compleat the works of death, desolation and tyranny, already begun with circumstances of Cruelty & perfidy scarcely parallel in the most barbarous ages, and totally unworthy the Head of a civilized nation.

He has constrained our fellow Citizens taken Captive on the high Seas to bear Arms against their Country, to become the executioners of their friends and Brethren, or to fall themselves by their Hands.

He has excited domestic insurrections amongst us, and has endeavoured to bring on the inhabitants of our frontiers, the merciless Indian Savages, whose known rule of warfare, is an undistinguished destruction of all ages, sexes and conditions.

In every stage of these Oppressions We have Petitioned for Redress in the most humble terms: Our repeated Petitions have been answered only by repeated injury. A Prince, whose character is thus marked by every act which may define a Tyrant, is unfit to be the ruler of a free People.

Nor have We been wanting in attention to our British brethren. We have warned them from time to time of attempts by their legislature to extend an unwarrantable jurisdiction over us. We have reminded them of the circumstances of our emigration and settlement here. We have appealed to their native justice and magnanimity, and we have conjured them by the ties of our common kindred to disavow these usurpations, which would inevitably interrupt our connections and correspondence. They too have been deaf to the voice of justice and of consanguinity. We must, therefore, acquiesce in the necessity, which denounces our Separation, and hold them, as we hold the rest of mankind, Enemies in War, in Peace Friends.

We, therefore, the Representatives of the united States of America, in General Congress, Assembled, appealing to the Supreme Judge of the world for the rectitude of our intentions, do, in the Name, and by Authority of the good People of these Colonies, solemnly publish and declare, That these United Colonies are, and of Right ought to be Free and Independent States; that they are Absolved from all Allegiance to the British Crown, and that all political connection between them and the State of Great Britain, is and ought to be totally dissolved; and that as Free and Independent States, they have full Power to levy War, conclude Peace, contract Alliances, establish Commerce, and to do all other Acts and Things which Independent States may of right do. And for the support of this Declaration, with a firm reliance on the Protection of Divine Providence, we mutually pledge to each other our Lives, our Fortunes and our sacred Honor.

CONSTITUTION OF THE UNITED STATES

We the People of the United States, in Order to form a more perfect Union, establish Justice, insure domestic Tranquility, provide for the common defence, promote the general Welfare, and secure the Blessings of Liberty to ourselves and our Posterity, do ordain and establish this CONSTITUTION for the United States of America.

ARTICLE I.

Section 1. All legislative Powers herein granted shall be vested in a Congress of the United States, which shall consist of a Senate and House of Representatives.

Section 2. The House of Representatives shall be composed of Members chosen every second Year by the People of the several States, and the Electors in each State shall have the Qualification requisite for Electors of the most numerous Branch of the State Legislature.

No Person shall be a Representative who shall not have attained to the Age of twenty-five Years, and been seven Years a Citizen of the United States, and who shall not, when elected, be an Inhabitant of that State in which he shall be chosen.

Representatives and direct Taxes shall be apportioned among the several States which may be included within this Union, according to their respective Numbers, which shall be determined by adding to the whole Number of free Persons, including those bound to Service for a Term of Years, and excluding Indians not taxed, three-fifths of all other Persons. The actual Enumeration shall be made within three Years after the first meeting of the Congress of the United States, and within every subsequent Term of ten Years, in such Manner as they shall by Law direct. The Number of Representatives shall not exceed one for every thirty Thousand, but each State shall have at Least one Representative; and until such enumeration shall be made, the State of New Hampshire shall be entitled to chuse three, Massachusetts eight, Rhode Island and Providence Plantations one, Connecticut five, New York six, New Jersey four, Pennsylvania eight, Delaware one, Maryland six, Virginia ten, North Carolina five, South Carolina five, and Georgia three.

When vacancies happen in the Representation from any State, the Executive Authority thereof shall issue Writs of Election, to fill such Vacancies.

The House of Representatives shall chuse their Speaker and other Officers; and shall have the sole Power of Impeachment.

Section 3. The Senate of the United States shall be composed of two Senators from each State, chosen by the Legislatures thereof, for six Years; and each Senator shall have one Vote.

Immediately after they shall be assembled in Consequence of the first Election, they shall be divided as equally as may be into three Classes. The Seats of the Senators of the first Class shall be vacated at the Expiration of the second Year, of the second Class at the Expiration of the fourth Year, and of the third Class at the Expiration of the sixth Year, so that one-third may be chosen every second Year; and if Vacancies happen by Resignation, or otherwise, during the Recess of the Legislature of any State, the Executive thereof may make temporary Appointments (until the next Meeting of the Legislature, which shall then fill such Vacancies).

No Person shall be a Senator who shall not have attained to the Age of thirty Years, and been nine Years a Citizen of the United States, and who shall not, when elected, be an Inhabitant of that State for which he shall be chosen.

The Vice President of the United States shall be President of the Senate, but shall have no Vote, unless they be equally divided.

The Senate shall chuse their other Officers, and also a President pro tempore, in the absence of the Vice President, or when he shall exercise the Office of President of the United States.

The Senate shall have the sole Power to try all Impeachments. When sitting for that Purpose, they shall be on Oath or Affirmation. When the President of the United States is tried, the Chief Justice shall preside: And no Person shall be convicted without the Concurrence of two-thirds of the Members present.

Judgment in Cases of Impeachment shall not extend further than to removal from Office, and disqualification to hold and enjoy any Office of honor, Trust or Profit under the United States: but the Party convicted shall nevertheless be liable and subject to Indictment, Trial, Judgment and Punishment, according to Law.

Section 4.   The Times, Places and Manner of holding Elections for Senators and Representatives, shall be prescribed in each State by the Legislature thereof; but the Congress may at any time by Law make or alter such Regulations, except as to the Places of chusing Senators.

The Congress shall assemble at least once in every Year, and such Meeting shall be on the first Monday in December, unless they shall by Law appoint a different Day.

Section 5.   Each House shall be the Judge of the Elections, Returns and Qualifications of its own Members, and a Majority of each shall constitute a Quorum to do Business; but a smaller Number may adjourn from day to day, and may be authorized to compel the Attendance of absent Members, in such Manner, and under such Penalties as each House may provide.

Each House may determine the Rules of its Proceedings, punish its Members for disorderly Behavior, and, with the Concurrence of two-thirds, expel a Member.

Each House shall keep a Journal of its Proceedings, and from time to time publish the same, excepting such Parts as may in their Judgment require Secrecy; and the Yeas and Nays of the Members of either House on any question shall, at the Desire of one-fifth of those Present, be entered on the Journal.

Neither House, during the Session of Congress, shall, without the Consent of the other, adjourn for more than three days, nor to any other Place than that in which the two Houses shall be sitting.

Section 6.   The Senators and Representatives shall receive a Compensation for their Services, to be ascertained by Law, and paid out of the Treasury of the United States.   They shall in all Cases, except Treason, Felony and Breach of the Peace, be privileged from Arrest during their Attendance at the Session of their respective Houses, and in going to and returning from the same; and for any Speech or Debate in either House, they shall not be questioned in any other Place.

No Senator or Representative shall, during the Time for which he was elected, be appointed to any civil Office under the Authority of the United States, which shall have been created, or the Emoluments whereof shall have been increased during such time; and no Person holding any Office under the United States, shall be a Member of either House during his Continuance in Office.

Section 7.   All Bills for raising Revenue shall originate in the House of Representatives; but the Senate may propose or concur with Amendments as on other Bills.

Every Bill which shall have passed the House of Representatives and the Senate, shall, before it become a Law, be presented to the President of the United States.   If he approve he shall sign it, but if not, he shall return it, with his Objections to that House in which it shall have originated, who shall enter the Objections at large on their Journal, and proceed to reconsider it.   If after such Reconsideration two thirds of that House shall agree to pass the Bill, it shall be sent, together with the Objections, to the other House, by which it shall likewise be reconsidered, and if approved by two thirds of that House, it shall become a Law.   But in all such Cases the Votes of both Houses shall be determined by Yeas and Nays, and the Names of the Persons voting for and against the Bill shall be entered on the Journal of each House respectively.   If any Bill shall not be returned by the President within ten Days (Sundays excepted) after it shall have been presented to him, the Same shall be a Law, in like Manner as if he had signed it, unless the Congress by their Adjournment prevent its Return, in which Case it shall not be a Law.

Every Order, Resolution, or Vote to which the Concurrence of the Senate and House of Representatives may be necessary (except on a question of Adjournment) shall be presented to the President of the United States; and before the Same shall take Effect, shall be approved by him, or being disapproved by him, shall be repassed by two thirds of the Senate and House of Representatives, according to the Rules and Limitations prescribed in the Case of a Bill.

Section 8.   The Congress shall have Power to lay and collect Taxes, Duties, Imposts and Excises, to pay the Debts and provide for the common Defence and general Welfare of the United States; but all Duties, Imposts and Excises shall be uniform throughout the United States;

To borrow money on the credit of the United States;

To regulate Commerce with foreign Nations, and among the Several States, and with the Indian Tribes;

To establish an uniform Rule of Naturalization, and uniform Laws on the subject of Bankruptcies throughout the United States;

To coin Money, regulate the Value thereof, and of foreign Coin, and fix the Standard of Weights and Measures;

To provide for the Punishment of counterfeiting the Securities and current Coin of the United States;

To establish Post Offices and post Roads;

To promote the Progress of Science and useful Arts, by securing for limited Times to Authors and Inventors the exclusive Right to their respective Writings and Discoveries;

To constitute Tribunals inferior to the supreme Court;

To define and punish Piracies and Felonies committed on the high Seas and Offences against the Law of Nations;

To declare War, grant Letters of Marque and Reprisal, and make Rules concerning Captures on Land and Water;

To raise and support Armies, but no Appropriation of Money to that Use shall be for a longer Term than two Years;

To provide and maintain a Navy;

To make Rules for the Government and Regulation of the land and naval Forces;

To provide for calling forth the Militia to execute the Laws of the Union, suppress Insurrections and repel Invasions;

To provide for organizing, arming, and disciplining the Militia, and for governing such Part of them as may be employed in the Service of the United States, reserving to the States respectively, the Appointment of the Officers, and the Authority of training the Militia according to the discipline prescribed by Congress;

To exercise exclusive Legislation in all Cases whatsoever, over such District (not exceeding ten Miles square) as may, by Cession of particular States, and the acceptance of Congress, become the Seat of the Government of the United States, and to exercise like Authority over all Places purchased by the Consent of the Legislature of the State in which the Same shall be, for the Erection of Forts, Magazines, Arsenals, Dock-Yards and other needful Buildings;—And

To make all Laws which shall be necessary and proper for carrying into Execution the foregoing Powers, and all other Powers vested by this Constitution in the Government of the United States, or in any Department or Officer thereof.

Section 9. The Migration or Importation of such Persons as any of the States now existing shall think proper to admit, shall not be prohibited by the Congress prior to the Year one thousand eight hundred and eight, but a tax or duty may be imposed on such Importation, not exceeding ten dollars for each Person.

The Privilege of the Writ of Habeas Corpus shall not be suspended, unless when in Cases of Rebellion or Invasion the public Safety may require it.

No Bill of Attainder or ex post facto Law shall be passed.

No Capitation, or other direct Tax shall be laid, unless in Proportion to the Census or Enumeration herein before directed to be taken.

No tax or Duty shall be laid on Articles exported from any State.

No Preference shall be given by any Regulation of Commerce or Revenue to the Ports of one State over those of another; nor shall Vessels bound to, or from, one State, be obliged to enter, clear, or pay Duties in another.

No Money shall be drawn from the Treasury, but in Consequence of Appropriations made by Law; and a regular Statement and Account of the Receipts and Expenditures of all Public Money shall be published from time to time.

No Title of Nobility shall be granted by the United States: And no Person holding any Office of Profit or Trust under them, shall, without the Consent of the Congress, accept of any present, Emolument, Office, or Title, of any kind whatever, from any King, Prince, or Foreign State.

Section 10. No State shall enter into any Treaty, Alliance, or Confederation; grant Letters of Marque and Reprisal; coin Money; emit Bills of Credit; make anything but gold and silver Coin a Tender in Payment of Debts; pass any Bill of Attainder, ex post facto law, or Law impairing the Obligation of Contracts, or grant any Title of Nobility.

No State shall, without the Consent of the Congress, lay any Imposts or Duties on Imports or Exports, except what may be absolutely necessary for executing its inspection Laws: and the net Produce of all Duties and Imposts, laid by any State on Imports or Exports, shall be for the Use of the Treasury of the United States; and all of such Laws shall be subject to the Revision and Control of the Congress.

No State shall, without the Consent of Congress, lay any duty of Tonnage, keep Troops, or Ships of War in time of Peace, enter into any Agreement or Compact with another State, or with a foreign Power, or engage in War, unless actually invaded, or in such imminent Danger as will not admit of Delay.

ARTICLE II.

The executive Power shall be vested in a President of the United States of America. He shall hold his Office during the Term of Four Years, and, together with the Vice President, chosen for the same Term, be elected, as follows

Each State shall appoint, in such Manner as the Legislature thereof may direct, a Number of Electors, equal to the whole Number of Senators and Representatives to which the State may be entitled in the Congress: but no Senator or Representative, or person holding an Office of Trust or Profit under the United States, shall be appointed an Elector.

The Electors shall meet in their respective States, and vote by Ballot for two persons, of whom one at least shall not be an Inhabitant of the same State with themselves. And they shall make a List of all the Persons voted for, and of the Number of Votes for each; which List they shall sign and certify, and transmit sealed to the Seat of the Government of the United States, directed to the President of the Senate. The President of the Senate shall, in the Presence of the Senate and House of Representatives, open all the Certificates, and the Votes shall then be counted. The Person having the greatest Number of Votes shall be the President, if such Number be a Majority of the whole Number of Electors appointed; and if there be more than one who have such Majority, and have an equal Number of Votes, then the House of Representatives shall immediately chuse by Ballot one of them for President; and if no Person have a Majority, then from the five highest on the List the said House shall in like Manner chuse the President. But in chusing the President, the Votes shall be taken by States, the Representation from each State having one Vote; A quorum for this Purpose shall consist of a Member or Members from two-thirds of the States, and a Majority of all the States shall be necessary to a Choice. In every Case, After the Choice of the President, the Person having the greatest number of Votes of the Electors shall be the Vice President. But if there should remain two or more who have equal Votes, the Senate shall chuse from them by Ballot the Vice President.

The Congress may determine the Time of chusing the Electors, and the Day on which they shall give their Votes; which Day shall be the same throughout the United States.

No person except a natural born Citizen, or a Citizen of the United States, at the time of the Adoption of this Constitution, shall be eligible to the Office of President; neither shall any Person be eligible to that Office who shall not have attained the age of thirty-five years, and been fourteen Years a Resident within the United States.

In Case of the Removal of the President from Office, or of his Death, Resignation or Inability to discharge the Powers and Duties of said Office, the Same shall devolve on the Vice President, and the Congress may by Law provide for the Case of Removal, Death, Resignation, or

Inability, both of the President and Vice President, declaring what Officer shall then act as President, and such Officer shall act accordingly, until the Disability be removed, or a President shall be elected.

The President shall, at stated Times, receive for his Services, a Compensation, which shall neither be increased nor diminished during the Period for which he shall have been elected, and he shall not receive within that Period any other Emolument from the United States, or any of them.

Before he enter on the Execution of his Office, he shall take the following Oath or Affirmation:—"I do solemnly swear (or affirm) that I will faithfully execute the Office of President of the United States, and will to the best of my Ability, preserve, protect and defend the Constitution of the United States."

Section 2. The President shall be Commander in Chief of the Army and Navy of the United States, and of the Militia of the several States, when called into the actual Service of the United States; he may require the Opinion, in writing, of the principal Officer in each of the executive Departments, upon any Subject relating to the Duties of their respective Offices, and he shall have Power to grant Reprieves and Pardons for Offences against the United States, except in Cases of Impeachment.

He shall have Power, by and with the Advice and Consent of the Senate, to make Treaties, provided two thirds of the Senators present concur; and he shall nominate, and by and with the Advice and Consent of the Senate, shall appoint Ambassadors, other public Ministers and Consuls, Judges of the supreme Court, and all other Officers of the United States, whose Appointments are not herein otherwise provided for, and which shall be established by Law: but the Congress may by Law vest the Appointment of such inferior Officers, as they think proper, in the President alone, in the Courts of Law, or in the Heads of Departments.

The President shall have Power to fill up all Vacancies that may happen during the recess of the Senate, by granting Commissions which shall expire at the End of their next Session.

Section 3. He shall from time to time give to the Congress Information of the state of the Union, and recommend to their Consideration such Measures as he shall judge necessary and expedient; he may, on extraordinary Occasions, convene both Houses, or either of them, and in Case of Disagreement between them, with Respect to the Time of Adjournment, he may adjourn them to such Time as he shall think proper; he shall receive Ambassadors and other public Ministers; he shall take Care that the Laws be faithfully executed, and shall Commission all the Officers of the United States.

Section 4. The President, Vice President and all civil Officers of the United States, shall be removed from Office on Impeachment for, and Conviction of, Treason, Bribery, or other high Crimes and Misdemeanors.

ARTICLE III.

Section 1. The judicial Power of the United States shall be vested in one supreme Court, and in such inferior Courts as the Congress may from time to time ordain and establish. The Judges, both of the supreme and inferior Courts, shall hold their Offices during good Behaviour, and shall, at stated Times, receive for their Services, a Compensation which shall not be diminished during their Continuance in Office.

Section 2.   The judicial Power shall extend to all Cases, in Law and Equity, arising under this Constitution, the Laws of the United States, and Treaties made, or which shall be made, under their Authority ;—to all Cases affecting Ambassadors, other public Ministers and Consuls ;—to all Cases of admiralty and maritime Jurisdiction ;—to Controversies to which the United States, shall be a party ;—to Controversies between two or more States ;—between a State and Citizens of another State ;—between Citizens of different States ;—between Citizens of the same State claiming Lands under Grants of different States, and between a State, or the Citizens thereof, and foreign States, Citizens or Subjects.

In all Cases affecting Ambassadors, other public Ministers and Consuls, and those in which a State shall be a Party, the supreme Court shall have original Jurisdiction.   In all the other Cases before mentioned, the supreme Court shall have appellate Jurisdiction, both as to Law and Fact, with such Exceptions, and under such Regulations as the Congress shall make.

The trial of all Crimes, except in Cases of Impeachment, shall be by Jury, and such Trial shall be held in the State where the said Crimes shall have been committed ; but when not committed within any State, the Trial shall be at such Place or Places as the Congress may by Law have directed.

Section 3.   Treason against the United States, shall consist only in levying War against them, or in adhering to their Enemies, giving them Aid and Comfort.   No person shall be convicted of Treason unless on the Testimony of two Witnesses to the same overt Act, or on Confession in open Court.

The Congress shall have power to declare the Punishment of Treason, but no Attainder of Treason shall work Corruption of Blood, or Forfeiture except during the Life of the Person attainted.

ARTICLE IV.

Section 1.   Full Faith and Credit shall be given in each State to the public Acts, Records and judicial Proceedings of every other State.   And the Congress may by general Laws prescribe the Manner in which such Acts, Records and Proceedings shall be proved, and the Effect thereon.

Section 2.   The Citizens of each State shall be entitled to all Privileges and Immunities of Citizens in the several States.

A Person charged in any State with Treason, Felony, or other Crime, who shall flee from Justice, and be found in another State, shall on demand of the executive Authority of the State from which he fled, be delivered up, to be removed to the State having Jurisdiction of the Crime.

No Person held to Service or Labour in one State, under the Laws thereof, escaping into another, shall, in Consequence of any Law or Regulation therein, be discharged from such service or Labour, but shall be delivered up on Claim of the Party to whom such Service or Labour may be due.

Section 3.   New States may be admitted by the Congress into this Union ; but no new State shall be formed or erected within the Jurisdiction of any other State ; nor any State be formed by the Junction of two or more States, or parts of States, without the Consent of the Legislatures of the States concerned as well as of the Congress.

The Congress shall have Power to dispose of and make all needful Rules and Regulations respecting the Territory or other property belonging to the United States; and nothing in this Constitution shall be so construed as to Prejudice any Claims of the United States, or of any particular State.

Section 4. The United States shall guarantee to every State in this Union a Republican Form of Government, and shall protect each of them against invasion; and on Application of the Legislature, or of the Executive (when the Legislature cannot be convened) against domestic Violence.

ARTICLE V.

The Congress, whenever two thirds of both Houses shall deem it necessary, shall propose Amendments to this Constitution, or, on the Application of the Legislatures of two thirds of the several States, shall call a Convention for proposing Amendments, which, in either Case, shall be valid to all Intents and Purposes, as Part of this Constitution, when ratified by the Legislatures of three-fourths of the several States, or by Conventions in three-fourths thereof, as the one or the other Mode of Ratification may be proposed by the Congress; Provided that no Amendment which may be made prior to the Year One thousand eight hundred and eight shall in any Manner affect the first and fourth Clauses in the Ninth Section of the first Article; and that no State, without its Consent, shall be deprived of its equal Suffrage in the Senate.

ARTICLE VI.

All Debts contracted and Engagements entered into, before the Adoption of this Constitution, shall be as valid against the United States under this Constitution, as under the Confederation.

This Constitution, and the Laws of the United States which shall be made in Pursuance thereof; and all Treaties made, or which shall be made, under the Authority of the United States, shall be the supreme Law of the Land; and the Judges in every State shall be bound thereby, any Thing in the Constitution or Laws of any State to the Contrary notwithstanding.

The Senators and Representatives before mentioned, and the Members of the several State Legislatures, and all executive and judicial Officers, both of the United States and of the several States, shall be bound by Oath or Affirmation, to support this Constitution; but no religious Test shall ever be required as a Qualification to any Office or public Trust under the United States.

ARTICLE VII.

The Ratification of the Conventions of nine States shall be sufficient for the Establishment of this Constitution between the States so ratifying the Same.

DONE in Convention by the Unanimous Consent of the States present the Seventeenth Day of September in the Year of our Lord one thousand seven hundred and Eighty seven, and of the Independence of the United States of America the Twelfth. In Witness whereof We have hereunto subscribed our Names,

Go. Washington
Presidt. and Deputy from Virginia.

ARTICLES IN ADDITION TO, AND AMENDMENT OF THE CONSTITUTION OF THE UNITED STATES OF AMERICA, PROPOSED BY CONGRESS, AND RATIFIED BY THE LEGISLATURES OF THE SEVERAL STATES PURSUANT TO THE FIFTH ARTICLE OF THE ORIGINAL CONSTITUTION.

ARTICLE I.

Congress shall make no law respecting an establishment of religion, or prohibiting the free exercise thereof; or abridging the freedom of speech, or of the press; or the right of the people peaceably to assemble, and to petition the Government for a redress of grievances.

ARTICLE II.

A well regulated Militia, being necessary to the security of a free State, the right of the people to keep and bear Arms, shall not be infringed.

ARTICLE III.

No Soldier shall, in time of peace, be quartered in any house, without the consent of the Owner, nor in time of war, but in a manner to be prescribed by law.

ARTICLE IV.

The right of the people to be secure in their persons, houses, papers, and effects, against unreasonable searches and seizures, shall not be violated, and no Warrants shall issue, but upon probable cause, supported by Oath or affirmation, and particularly describing the place to be searched, and the persons or things to be seized.

ARTICLE V.

No person shall be held to answer for a capital, or otherwise infamous crime, unless on a presentment or indictment of a Grand Jury, except in cases arising in the land or naval forces, or in the Militia, when in actual service in time of War or public danger; nor shall any person be subject for the same offence to be twice put in jeopardy of life or limb; nor shall be compelled in any criminal case to be a witness against himself, nor be deprived of life, liberty, or property, without due process of law; nor shall private property be taken for public use, without just compensation.

ARTICLE VI.

In all criminal prosecutions, the accused shall enjoy the right to a speedy and public trial, by an impartial jury of the State and district wherein the crime shall have been committed, which district shall have been previously ascertained by law, and to be informed of the nature and cause of the accusation; to be confronted with the witnesses against him; to have compulsory process for obtaining witnesses in his favor, and to have the Assistance of Counsel for his defence.

ARTICLE VII.

In suits at common law, where the value in controversy shall exceed twenty dollars, the right of trial by jury shall be preserved, and no fact tried by a jury shall be otherwise re-examined in any Court of the United States, than according to the rules of the common law.

ARTICLE VIII.

Excessive bail shall not be required, nor excessive fines imposed, nor cruel and unusual punishments inflicted.

ARTICLE IX.

The enumeration in the Constitution, of certain rights, shall not be construed to deny or disparage others retained by the people.

ARTICLE X.

The powers not delegated to the United States by the Constitution, nor prohibited by it to the States, are reserved to the States respectively, or to the people.

ARTICLE XI.

The Judicial power of the United States shall not be construed to extend to any suit in law or equity, commenced or prosecuted against one of the United States by Citizens of another State, or by Citizens or Subjects of any Foreign State.

ARTICLE XII.

The Electors shall meet in their respective states and vote by ballot for President and Vice-President, one of whom, at least, shall not be an inhabitant of the same state with themselves; they shall name in their ballots the person voted for as President, and in distinct ballots the person voted for as Vice-President, and they shall make distinct lists of all persons voted for as President, and of all persons voted for as Vice-President, and of the number of votes for each, which lists they shall sign and certify, and transmit sealed to the seat of the government of the United States, directed to the President of the Senate;—The President of the Senate shall, in presence of the Senate and House of Representatives, open all the certificates and the votes shall then be counted;—The person having the greatest number of votes for President, shall be the President, if such number be a majority of the whole number of Electors appointed; and if no person have such majority, then from the persons having the highest numbers not exceeding three on the list of those voted for as President, the House of Representatives shall choose immediately, by ballot, the President. But in choosing the President, the votes shall be taken by states, the representation from each state having one vote; a quorum for this purpose shall consist of a member or members from two-thirds of the states, and a majority of all the states shall be necessary to a choice. And if the House of Representatives shall not choose a President whenever the right of choice shall devolve upon them, before the fourth day of March next following, then the

Vice-President shall act as President, as in the case of the death or other constitutional disability of the President.—The person having the greatest number of votes as Vice-President, shall be the Vice-President, if such number be a majority of the whole number of Electors appointed, and if no person, have a majority, then from the two highest numbers on the list, the Senate shall choose the Vice-President; a quorum for the purpose shall consist of two-thirds of the whole number of Senators, and a majority of the whole number shall be necessary to a choice. But no person constitutionally ineligible to the office of President shall be eligible to that of Vice-President of the United States.

ARTICLE XIII.

Section 1.   Neither slavery nor involuntary servitude, except as a punishment for crime whereof the party shall have been duly convicted, shall exist within the United States, or any place subject to their jurisdiction.

Section 2.   Congress shall have power to enforce this article by appropriate legislation.

ARTICLE XIV.

Section 1.   All persons born or naturalized in the United States, and subject to the jurisdiction thereof, are citizens of the United States and of the State wherein they reside. No State shall make or enforce any law which shall abridge the privileges or immunities of citizens of the United States; nor shall any State deprive any person of life, liberty, or property, without due process of law; nor deny to any person within its jurisdiction the equal protection of the laws.

Section 2.   Representatives shall be apportioned among the several States according to their respective numbers, counting the whole number of persons in each State, excluding Indians not taxed. But when the right to vote at any election for the choice of electors for President and Vice-President of the United States, Representatives in Congress, the Executive and Judicial officers of a State, or the members of the Legislature thereof, is denied to any of the male inhabitants of such State, being twenty-one years of age, and citizens of the United States, or in any way abridged, except for participation in rebellion, or other crime, the basis of representation therein shall be reduced in the proportion which the number of such male citizens shall bear to the whole number of male citizens twenty-one years of age in such State.

Section 3.   No person shall be a Senator or Representative in Congress, or elector of President and Vice-President, or hold any office, civil or military, under the United States, or under any State, who, having previously taken an oath, as a member of Congress, or as an officer of the United States, or as a member of any State Legislature, or as an executive or judicial officer of any State, to support the Constitution of the United States, shall have engaged in insurrection or rebellion against the same, or given aid or comfort to the enemies thereof. But Congress may, by a vote of two-thirds of each House, remove such disability.

Section 4.   The validity of the public debt of the United States, authorized by law, including debts incurred for payment of pensions and bounties for services in suppressing insurrection or rebellion, shall not be questioned. But neither the United States nor any other State shall assume to pay any debt or obligation incurred in aid of insurrection or rebellion against the United States, or any claim for the loss or emancipation of any slave; but all such debts, obligations and claims shall be held illegal and void.

Section 5. The Congress shall have power to enforce, by appropriate legislation, the provisions of this article.

ARTICLE XV.

Section 1. The right of citizens of the United States to vote shall not be denied or abridged by the United States or by any State on account of race, color, or previous condition of servitude.

Section 2. The Congress shall have power to enforce this article by appropriate legislation.

ARTICLE XVI.

The Congress shall have power to lay and collect taxes on incomes, from whatever source derived, without apportionment among the several States, and without regard to any census or enumeration.

ARTICLE XVII.

The Senate of the United States shall be composed of two Senators from each State, elected by the people thereof, for six years; and each Senator shall have one vote. The electors in each State shall have the qualifications requisite for electors of the most numerous branch of the State legislatures.

When vacancies happen in the representation of any State in the Senate, the executive authority of such State shall issue writs of election to fill such vacancies: Provided, That the legislature of any State may empower the executive thereof to make temporary appointment until the people fill the vacancies by election as the legislature may direct.

This amendment shall not be so construed as to affect the election or term of any Senator chosen before it becomes valid as part of the Constitution.

ARTICLE XVIII.

Section 1. After one year from the ratification of this article the manufacture, sale, or transportation of intoxicating liquors within, the importation thereof into, or the exportation thereof from the United States and all territory subject to the jurisdiction thereof for beverage purposes is hereby prohibited.

Section 2. The Congress and the several States shall have concurrent power to enforce this article by appropriate legislation.

Section 3. This article shall be inoperative unless it shall have been ratified as an amendment to the Constitution by the legislatures of the several States, as provided in the Constitution, within seven years from the date of the submission hereof to the States by the Congress.

ARTICLE XIX.

The right of citizens of the United States to vote shall not be denied or abridged by the United States or by any State on account of sex.

Congress shall have power to enforce this article by appropriate legislation.